The Pubhiker's Guide:
Real Walks – Real Ale!

Mick Payne

Published by Sigma Leisure – an imprint of
Sigma Press, 1 South Oak Lane, Wilmslow, Cheshire SK9 6AR, England.

British Library Cataloguing in Publication Data
A CIP record for this book is available from the British Library.

ISBN: 1-85058-566-0

Typesetting and Design by: Sigma Press, Wilmslow, Cheshire.

Cover photograph: Linda Payne at The Snake Pass Inn *(Mick Payne)*

Maps and photographs: the author

Printed by: MFP Design and Print

PREFACE

This is a book of great variety. The variety of the hills of England and Wales combined with that of Traditional Beer and the pubs that serve it. From the soft Millstone Grit of the Southern Pennines to the diamond hard quartzite of the Stiperstones in Shropshire's secret hills, it marries walks on high hills and moorland with welcoming pubs. There are well-known walks starting from famous villages, but there is also a good leavening of unusual, perhaps even idiosyncratic, outings that will probably be new to most people.

The beer available in the pubs that are featured has as great a regional variation as the landscape itself. Many local and independent brewers depend on water that has filtered though the very rock that we walk on; for that reason, where a choice in pubs may be offered by a particular location, I have tended to lean towards the outlet favouring local breweries.

For the more experienced walker, requiring more than a stroll from a country pub, this book, I hope offers the answer: walks from about 5 to 15 miles visiting *en route* the high moors and hills of the Pennines; the fells of the English Lake District; Snowdon by a less popular yet still satisfying route; and the little-visited Shropshire Hills. There are routes for most abilities of hill-walker (the chapters are laid out in ascending order of difficulty), although I hope that even Himalayan veterans will find the routes as enjoyable as I have.

Finally, what can be more agreeable part-way round a walk, or after a day on the hills, than relaxing in a pub with a glass of local beer? In summer, perhaps the pleasures of tracing one's route from a sunlit garden, whilst in winter, roasting in front of a real fire while cradling a glass of dark, seasonal ale. The pleasure is there for the taking.

Acknowledgements

Thanks to the following people who have helped check routes, provided information or just given encouragement: my wife Linda; Tara, our Real Ale loving dog; Alan and Rita Howkins; George and Linda Reed.

Mick Payne

Contents

Introduction

This is a very different type of pub walks book to those that have gone before. The emphasis is on both mountain and moorland. The uplands of England and Wales can be wild and dramatic places, and this small volume has walks in many of the best-known hill areas. The main requirements are that the countryside has to reach a height around the 1000ft contour together with a reasonably feeling of remoteness. I make no apologies for sticking to feet for the heights on the maps, though I also assume that the reader will be using a modern metric OS map.

Because of the more serious aspect of the walks, there are certain recommended minimums required in the way of equipment and even personal experience. The sterner the landscape, the more this is so. The potential for bad weather increases in these uplands, and the people who, even in summer, set off on a moorland or mountain walk without reasonable clothing and footwear do so at their own risk. With Britain's notoriously changeable climate hypothermia is an ever-present hazard, even in summer. Wax cotton jackets and green wellies may be adequate two miles from a lowland pub, but they have no place in the higher hills.

It is not necessary to equip yourself for a Himalayan expedition, especially when attempting the easier walks in this book. But a basic kit of boots, waterproofs and a rucksack is a good idea and one that will form the foundation for a lifetime's walking the hill paths of Britain.

First and foremost is a good pair of walking boots. Even the easiest and shortest routes, such as Derbyshire's Eastern Edges, will often have damp or boggy sections and rocky going is almost a certainty. These may be leather, fabric, suede or totally synthetic in construction, but should in any case have a degree of stiffness in the sole, allied with a modicum of support for the ankle. For the higher and more serious walks, such as Lakeland's Blencathra, a more substantial boot is recommended, although it is not to say that in good conditions lighter footwear will be inadequate.

For walking in any other than heat-wave conditions a few specialised items of clothing are going to be necessary. A waterproof jacket and over-trousers are the basic minimum, preferably breathable, so that it can be worn purely to keep out the wind, even when it is not raining. Do not, however, expect the same degree of breathability when you are toiling uphill in a downpour.

For a middle layer, modern fleece garments take some beating. The tops are usually smart enough to wear as casual jackets, whilst fleece bottoms will keep the legs warm in the coldest conditions; ordinary stretch tracksuit type bottoms being good enough for milder weather. Next to the skin it is best to wear a purpose-made base layer, as they wick perspiration away from the body, enabling the other layers to operate at maximum efficiency.

As most of the walks are longer and more serious than the average found in pub walk books some food is going to be necessary, even if only for emergencies. To this end it is a good idea to keep a supply of high energy foods in your rucksack at all times, along with a first aid kit, a torch and a whistle. The last is for making the recognised distress call – six short blasts in succession, followed by a one minute pause, then repeat – in case of an accident (after dark, the same pattern is followed with torch flashes). Also, especially for the higher and more remote walks, a compass – and the knowledge of how to use it – is a necessity, along with the relevant large scale maps for the area (the sketch maps in this book are for guidance only, and are based upon my own interpretation of the terrain).

All the former guidelines assume that the walks will generally be undertaken in reasonably good weather. Winter conditions (which can occur at almost any time on the higher hills) can change things dramatically. An easy walk may become a battle against the elements in a very short time taking twice as long as envisaged, and a white-out on top of Snowdon is no place to practise navigation. To undertake any but the easiest walks under snow or ice conditions, it is advisable to take an ice axe; for some of the walks you may need crampons (and be familiar with their use), and you should carry extra clothing and food.

Listen to the local weather forecasts, and do not be afraid to amend or even abort the day if you think the conditions are beyond your capabilities. Remember that wind and altitude can quickly render a pleasant day in the valley to near Arctic conditions at just 2000 feet. It is better to pop a few coins into the mountain rescue collection box in the pub than meet the team in earnest on a freezing summit.

Access Notes

The walker in England and Wales has legal access to the countryside only on the various Public Rights of Way or in some cases, common land; all other access is to be taken as concessionary. Even in the National Parks, all the land belongs to someone and if you enter land on which there is no right of way and against the wishes of the landowner, then you are committing trespass.

The walker has a legal right to use Public Footpaths as well as Bridleways, and Byways Open to All Traffic. Furthermore, in many cases, blanket access such as that defined by the Access Agreement in the Peak District does exist. This, however, depends on good will, so it is necessary to follow the rules under which the access is offered; this is especially important in relation to dogs, which still do great damage to many sheep in upland areas each year.

The sketch maps relating to the walks are for information only and are drawn to give an idea to the walker of the type of terrain to expect. They do not show all available footpaths – generally only those which form the route, or may be used as short cuts – and are not meant to replace an OS map, which in mountain country is especially necessary. The recommended map details are shown in the area introductions and in the data panel of every walk.

As more people seek pleasure in hill walking each year it is especially important to observe the country code and leave the hills and fells how you would wish to find them.

The Country Code

- ¤ Enjoy the countryside and respect its life and work.
- ¤ Guard against risk of fire.
- ¤ Fasten all gates behind you.
- ¤ Keep dogs under strict control.
- ¤ Keep to public rights of way across farmland.
- ¤ Use gates and stiles to cross fences, hedges and walls.
- ¤ Leave livestock, crops and machinery alone.
- ¤ Take all your litter home.
- ¤ Do not pollute water.
- ¤ Protect wildlife, plants and trees.
- ¤ Make no unnecessary noise.

Note that there is no implied right regarding parking in the pub car parks during the day; alternative parking is usually indicated. Many publicans will be happy for potential customers to park, especially at less busy times, although this is up to the individual walker to check.

Whilst every care has been taken in the compilation of this book, changes do occur or mistakes may have been made and all information is, to the best of my knowledge, correct at the time of going to press. The author would be grateful for notification of any said changes, be they to the routes or the chosen pubs, c/o the publisher.

The Beer and the Pubs

Unlike most beers, cask conditioned – or bottle conditioned – beers are alive. This, the traditional form of beer, only became threatened at the beginning of the 1960s with the arrival of keg beers. These were brewed in much the same way, but the process was halted before the finished product was put into the cask or barrel. Herein lies the difference!

Real Ales, the generic term for all live beers, continue to ferment in whatever container they leave the brewery in, be it cask or bottle.

This allows the natural and complex flavours to develop, and continue developing throughout the beer's life. This causes complications: short shelf life, the need for racking and settling at the point of sale and, last but not least, a greater commitment from the publican.

Some modern beers are marketed as 'real', when they are just an updated version of the bad old kegs of the 60s. Using combinations of nitrogen and carbon dioxide, they give a less gassy result, and one much nearer to that of Real Ale. They are, however, dead! It is the presence of the gas that gives the beer its tight and creamy head, nothing to do with the yeast still working in the cask. For the purpose of this book they have been relegated to the position they deserve.

The pubs in this book have been chosen as much to tie in with walks as for the outright quality of their beer. They also have to be walker friendly, as well as preferably having an open mind on children and dogs. Food is not a requirement (although most of them now serve meals and snacks) but drinkable real ale is! Where there is a choice, I have generally tended to list pubs that do give the best ale in the area. This philosophy, however, still does not override the main aims of this book: a good walk, followed by a good pint. It's not much use listing a pub that will not tolerate normal walking gear!

One of the delights of recent years is the upsurge in micro-breweries. These small concerns spring up all over the place, often dependent on the local free-trade for their very existence. To this end, some pubs have been selected for their selection of local beers, although not at the expense of the beer being of a good, drinkable quality or of compromising any of the other parameters.

Finally, the pubs are my own choice, there have been no outside influences, other than that of my wife, our Real Ale drinking Alsatian and my friends, as to their inclusion. No doubt there will be disagreements with some choices, but at least you know there is a pub half way round, or at the end of a walk that will not throw you out for dripping rainwater on the carpet.

KEY TO MAPS

━━━━━━━━━━━━ MAJOR ROADS

━━━━━━━━━━━━ MINOR ROADS

─────────── PATHS

 PUB   LOCAL BREWERY

BUILDINGS

LAKES

WOODS

 TELEPHONE IN RURAL AREA    CHURCH OR CHAPEL

UPHILL

DOWNHILL

LEVEL WALKING

UNDULATING OR RIDGE WALKING

The Lake District

The Lake District is England's largest National Park (866 square miles), and is also one of the most popular. Within the confines of the park there are several distinct landscapes. There is a great difference from the Skiddaw Slates in the north, through the Borrowdale Volcanics in the centre to the Silurian Slate of the landscape around Lake Windermere, reflected in the shapes of the hills.

The northern mountains around the town of Keswick are mainly rounded with shaley slopes, such as Blencathra which is featured in walk 4, and Skiddaw, one of Lakeland's 3000-footers. Towards the centre, the hills become more rocky, with some airy walking along exposed ridges and some routes to the top are attainable only by mild scrambling. Here lies the delectable Langdale Valley with its proud Pikes and the impressive Crinkle Crags (see route 5), while just to the south are to be found the Coniston Group, high above the town of the same name.

Many of the walks in this section visit sites of long-gone industry. The oldest is on the northern slopes of the Langdale Pikes, in the form of a Prehistoric stone axe factory, while the fells of Coniston Old Man are honeycombed with mines dating from the copper industry, and all around are the scars of slate mining. Fortunately time has softened the impact of many of these locations, and that which remains only serves to add an extra dimension to the trip.

One of the great pleasures of Lake District walking is the ability to string together several hills within a one-day expedition, the linking of high ridges meaning that once up to a reasonable height it is seldom necessary to lose too much altitude to reach the next summit. Combine this with the often horseshoe-shaped valleys (said by Wordsworth to resemble the spokes of a wheel with the hub at Esk Hause) and it means that it is generally very convenient to return to the day's start point, not always easy in some hill areas, but a great bonus to the 'pubhiker'.

Inns and mountaineering have always gone hand in hand in the Lake District. It was to such places as Wasdale Head where the pioneers of the sport came in the Victorian era, and it is said that rock climbing was born in 1886 when W. P. Haskett-Smith climbed Nape's Needle. With such historic connections, and the fact that the Lakes have been a popular destination since tourism began with the railways really opening up the area, it is not surprising that the region is well served with pubs and hotels of all kinds.

Real ale is to be found almost everywhere, and there are six breweries within the county of Cumbria – that of Jennings being the best known, although many other North Country beers may be found. To complement the beer there are a few well-known climbers' bars, the most famous being the ancient and basic Old Dungeon Ghyll in Great Langdale, although because of the popularity of walking, and the sheer numbers taking part, most places are 'walker friendly' – a fine situation!

The maps required to cover all the walks in this section are OS Landranger (1:50 000) sheets 90 and 96.

Walk 1: A Loughrigg Traverse

Distance: 7.5 miles (12km)

Height gained: 1090ft (332m)

Time: 3 hours.

Start: Ambleside Car Park. GR 374047.

Terrain: Good paths to excellent viewpoint, with a return along the lakeside path.

Maps: OS Landranger Sheet 90 – Penrith & Keswick (1:50 000).

Public transport: Ambleside is very well served by buses.

The Golden Rule, Ambleside; tel: (015394) 32257

What do you do in The Lakes when it is raining? Go to the pub, of course! However, as this is a walking book, there has to be the occasional route for bad weather or short days. This is such a route, although the pub is an absolute gem too. The Golden Rule is a well known climbers' pub, perhaps the best known in the Lakes, and is everything a traditional pub should be. It is the area's most frequent CAMRA Good Beer Guide entry with its Robinson's and Hartley's beers. Need I say more?

Loughrigg

Loughrigg rises behind Ambleside in a sprawling, shapeless mass, but this does not mean that it is an unworthy expedition. Criss-crossed with paths and with many small outcrops and false summits it is a hill that has a surprise round every corner and one that repays leisurely exploration rewarded by the excellent views it enjoys, not just towards Derwent and Rydal Waters, but also across to Langdale and Elterwater. It is only 1101ft (335m) in height and the walk is one of the easiest in this book, but it has a definite mountain feel.

The Walk

From the car park walk back towards Ambleside and take Vicarage Road which is signposted to Rothay Park and Loughrigg. Pass to the right of St Mary's church and follow the metalled lane into Rothay Park, where the path leads past some amazing giant's Bonsai trees growing on rock outcrops. At the edge of the park cross the bridges out onto the lane and turn right then immediately left at a finger-post.

Level ground is now left behind – the advantage however, of the steepness being the speed with which the views over the surrounding fells open out. At least the surface is good! The track briefly levels out before climbing again alongside a wall, to a gate. Here the walk enters the open fellside and passes the cottage of Pine Rigg with its superb garden before a kissing gate brings another short rise. Leave the wall and meander across upland pastures on an obvious path to another sign to Loughrigg.

Drop to a small stream and follow the track to the right, scrambling over a few small outcrops, and into The Amphitheatre. Climb steeply up the left-hand side to a level path and a cairn with excellent views into Langdale. The obvious path is now cairned all the way, and drops first into a small, marshy depression, then climbs on a sometimes loose path to suddenly emerge at the trig point.

Continue in the same direction along the well-worn path with Dunmail Raise and Helm Crag in front. This soon leads to the cairn overlooking Grasmere with fine views all round, and the start of the steep descent. This is a manufactured path winding steadily down towards the lake and a few zig-zags and steps soon have you on the wide path of Loughrigg Terrace.

This is a virtually level, gravel track liberally supplied with seats which gives easy and uncomplicated walking all the way to the shores of Rydal Water. The path is broken, first by a small stream and stepping stones, then by a tiny buttress blocking the path to the water's edge. At a fork, take the lower branch via a gate into Rydal Wood, an Access Area, this then meanders through the woods on a good path, before re-emerging alongside the river at a wooden bridge. Cross this and climb to the road.

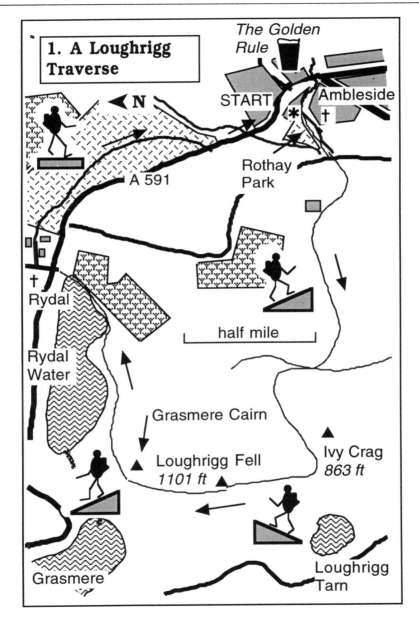

1. A Loughrigg Traverse

The Golden Rule

START

Ambleside

N

A 591

Rothay Park

half mile

Rydal

Rydal Water

Grasmere Cairn

Loughrigg Fell
1101 ft

Ivy Crag
863 ft

Grasmere

Loughrigg Tarn

Grasmere from Loughrigg

Turn right, then after a few metres left, along the road to Rydal Hall. Climb gently, then follow the sign again – this also now shows the way to a rambler's teashop – on through the cluster of buildings and out onto the park drive, crossing Rydal Beck. Easy and pleasant walking soon has the Scandale Beck joining from the left and the track follows its course before turning off rightwards to emerge onto the road at a pair of ornamental iron gates. Ambleside is now but a few minutes walk away, with the Golden Rule up the steep hill of Smithy Brow (the Kirkstone Road) just to the left.

Walk 2: Around Green Burn

Distance: 9.7 miles (15.5km)

Height gained: 2300ft (701m)

Time: 3.5 to 4.5 hours

Start: Grasmere Car Park. GR 336073.

Terrain: Easy paths over low fells, some boggy walking is inevitable beyond Calf Crag.

Maps: OS Landranger Sheet 90 – Penrith & Keswick (1:50 000).

Public transport: Grasmere is well served by buses.

The Traveller's Rest, Grasmere; tel: (015394) 35378

Just outside the honey pot village of Grasmere, and before the A591 starts its climb towards Dunmail Raise is the small, white painted Traveller's Rest. An excellent pub, it caters for the passing trade as well as locals and is a comfortable retreat at the end of a day's walking. It serves a range of Jennings beers and food in its varied bars or in the small garden with its attendant stream. Children and dogs (not in the restaurant) are welcome.

Helm Crag

Helm Crag is the hill that most visitors to the Lake District can identify. Almost everyone can recognise the rock formations atop the fell as The Lion and the Lamb – although which is which may be open to debate as the tourist's coaches speed away from Grasmere. It deserves better than that though, and this absolutely delightful walk sees that it gets it. Helm Crag is only 1299ft (396m) high, but it is a proper little mountain nonetheless, and when combined with Gibson Knott, a little higher at 1379ft (420m), Calf Crag and Steel Fell it is just the first step of an excellent round.

The Walk

From the car park in Grasmere village follow Broadgate then Easdale Road past the Butterlip How youth hostel – just beyond is a second car park, but an early start is required to secure a place – to a swing to the right and a signpost to Far Easdale, Borrowdale and more importantly for the Pubhiker, Helm Crag. After a gate, there are superb views of the waterfalls of Sour Milk Gill, then another wooden sign by a gate which leads onto a rougher path. Simply follow this to a sign to Helm Crag.

The path up Helm Crag is well engineered, and combined with the views into Far Easdale makes the walking a real pleasure. After a few zig-zags it traverses to the ridge overlooking Dunmail Raise and attacks the rocky top of the fell. From here to the summit all manner of little scrambles may be followed before emerging onto the rock-crowned crest with its, now apparently massive, rock

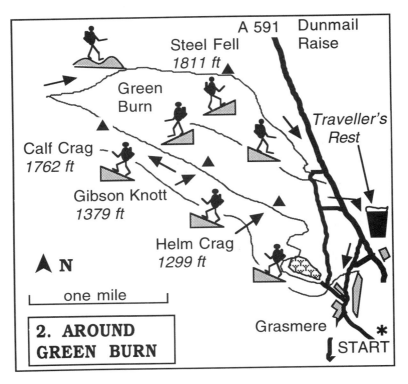

formations. The extent of the ridge is marked by the Lion and the Lamb at the Grasmere end, and a huge cantilevered rock, The Howitzer, at the other.

From the summit, the next section of the walk is obvious, but it is unfortunately necessary to lose about 300ft (91m) in the mile or so to Gibson Knott. From the col between the two, it is worth taking a glance back at Helm Crag as it looks most impressive, it also might help distract the mind from the juicy nature of the path. It can be wet . . . but worse is to come! It soon, however, contours the Easdale side of the fell, picking its way through tiny outcrops, and climbs to the knobby summit with its view on to Calf Crag.

Calf Crag is appreciably higher at 1762ft (537m) and just over a mile distant. This unfortunately starts by crossing a morass of black peat, although the path soon becomes better as it carves a rising traverse on the left of the ridge to find a way through the small summit crags. This is basically the end of the long ridge from Helm Crag, and the way now swings to the right to drop to the boggy hollow below Greenup Edge.

The path here is easy to follow as it follows the line of a broken fence. It is just as well that the navigation is easy, as on some parts flippers seem of more use than boots, and concentration is required to avoid wet feet. It is worth it though, as the path improves, so the views do too. Helvellyn in front, the ridge so recently quit to the right, and at the far end of St John's in the Vale the magnificent 'clenched fist' of Blencathra (Route 4). As height is gained the path gets better, now alongside a new fence, and eventually the 1811ft (552m) top of Steel Fell is reached.

This is the highest point of the walk, and the views have more than made up for the effort of getting here, but down it has to be. Facing Helm Crag, now well below, a feint path may be seen across the grassy top of the fell. This drops gently to a rocky band and a steepening, before returning to a more amiable rate of descent. It continues to drop in steps to a fork; go left, and continue to bracken clad slopes, a gap in the wall and a gate. A line of posts lead across pastures, then the path zig-zags towards the Green Burn.

Just before the stream is reached there is a National Trust sign and

Near the summit of Steel Fell, with Thirlmere and Blencathra in the background

a gate. Go through this and follow the track beyond to the road. Turn right and cross the bridge, a quiet and peaceful place to take a last look at the hills, then carry on turning left at the next junction, then onto the signposted footpath which leads to the Traveller's Rest.

With legs stiffening from the enforced rest, either send someone for the car and have another pint, or walk towards Grasmere for a few minutes and take the road just before the Swan Hotel – Pye Lane – then right, and back to Grasmere, where hopefully the Helm Crag spotting crowds will have gone on to 'see' something else.

Walk 3: The Langdale Pikes

Distance: 4.8 miles (7.7km)

Height gained: 2485ft (758m)

Time: 4 to 5 hours.

Start: Dungeon Ghyll car park. GR 295065.

Terrain: Good paths to four Langdale Pikes. High fells with one avoidable easy scramble, under snow and ice, this becomes a particularly serious undertaking often requiring full winter mountaineering equipment.

Maps: OS Landranger Sheet 90 – Penrith & Keswick (1:50 000).

Public transport: Fairly frequent buses run along Langdale.

The New Dungeon Ghyll Hotel, Great Langdale; tel: (015394) 37213

The New Dungeon Ghyll is the first of the climbers' hotels in the Langdale Valley to be reached. It backs directly onto the fellside, and the chosen route starts and finishes at its door. It is a Free House with a fair choice of beers, and there is a quiet walkers' bar in the hotel or the more animated Stickle Barn outside. Food is available at the usual times. Children and dogs are welcome and there is a large outdoor seating area to savour the views.

The Langdale Pikes

The Langdale Pikes make up the finest skyline in The Lakes. They appear to tower above the road in a way that belies their modest heights. They are all shapely mountains and close examination does nothing to lessen that opinion. Cut by the great ravine of Dungeon Ghyll and with the almost circular Stickle Tarn below Pavey Ark, the scenery is about as diverse as is possible in such a small area. The route as described takes in all four tops via Jack's Rake, an easy and safe scramble on Pavey Ark – this is *the* route to the top. It may, however, be avoided by two easier alternatives.

The Walk

There is a choice of two car parks at the foot of Dungeon Ghyll but the way is the same. Walk straight past the pub – plenty of time for a beer later – and take the wooden gate out onto the hillside. Ignore the obvious bridge and take instead the rising path round the back of the Stickle Barn. Rough at first it soon leads to a well made path climbing alongside the stream. About fifteen minutes steady walking reaches a bridge which is crossed to the opposite bank and the toil continues.

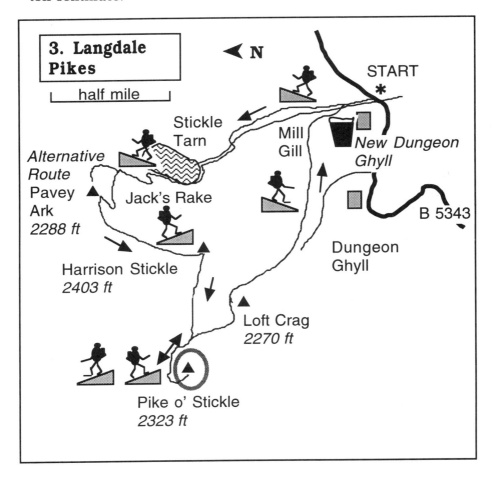

3. Langdale Pikes

half mile

◀ N

START
*

Stickle Tarn

Mill Gill

New Dungeon Ghyll

Alternative Route
Pavey Ark
2288 ft

Jack's Rake

B 5343

Harrison Stickle
2403 ft

Dungeon Ghyll

Loft Crag
2270 ft

Pike o' Stickle
2323 ft

High on Jack's Rake, above Stickle Tarn

The path climbs steadily on well made zig-zags with the upper section of Mill Gill to the left and Tarn Crag to the right. As it approaches the tarn the track gets increasingly rocky, until it may be necessary to resort to using hands as well as feet. Cross to the west bank of the stream again, and follow the still good path onwards. At the dam, the full majesty of Pavey Ark's crags burst into view. This is a pleasant, if sometimes crowded place to rest, while picking out the lines of ascent to the top of the fell.

The easiest is the blunt north flank that forms the right-hand skyline of the face providing an easy if comparatively tedious way up. Next in line is just to the left, East Gully. This is the sloping scree gully that slants from left to right, cutting off a section of the base of the crag. This is easy, although where the gully is blocked by chock-stones it provides a little amusement. This gains the previous route at about two-thirds height. The third, and by far the best way is the aforementioned Jack's Rake. This slopes right across the face from the base of East Gully at an angle of about 30° and although classed as a scramble is easy and secure, even though a head for heights is still an advantage.

Assuming the rake is to be taken, walk around the west shore of the tarn – this is also applicable for ascents of East Gully – where in a few minutes it is possible to climb the screes to the foot of the route. Here it is easy to assess the difficulties of Jack's Rake and to either commit to that, or take the easier East Gully option.

The path up the rake is immediately obvious, there are steep rocks above and below, while a worn runnel crosses the vast cliff to a tree and an obvious notch. At the tree, the right-hand wall begins to close in a little, snagging on your 'sac, and a few moves on good holds soon have the main difficulties passed. Following a short level section is another groove, then easy scrambling/walking leads enticingly across the face, giving a rare insight into the steep world of the rock climber. At the end of the rake proper, the path bears right and easy scrambling on huge holds leads straight to the summit wall of Pavey Ark. This is then followed easily to the top.

From Pavey Ark (2288ft, 697m), briefly retrace your steps and cross the marshy depression scattered with tiny tarns, to a wooden post marking the path to Harrison Stickle. A line of cairns may be followed leading straight to a shoulder of Harrison where an easy rocky ascent may be made to the summit (2403ft, 733 m, and the highest of the Langdale Pikes). The views from this lofty point are superb with the great bulk of Pavey Ark, so recently crossed, holding the gaze but also including Skiddaw, Helvellyn and Scafell Pike. Also may be seen the broad scar leading to the next objective – Pike o' Stickle.

Scramble easily down from the summit to the obvious path and cross the depression where rocks have been laid to help traverse any wet areas. If the path is followed westwards it comes, at an abrupt left turn to a deep gully, where easy scrambling soon leads to the perfect dome-shaped summit (2323ft, 708m) with magnificent views of Mickleden and Bowfell. The top may be left in a roughly north-eastwards direction where more easy scrambling over ledges and winding paths leads to the foot of the rocks. From the top of the large scree gully on the Mickleden face, take the fainter path branching off to the right. In a few minutes easy walking, with good views of Gimmer Crag, the top of Loft Crag (2270ft, 692m) is reached.

Everything from here is downhill (well, almost!) so take the path over the top and at a cairn down the left-hand side of the peak back towards Harrison Stickle. First on scree, then a peaty path, walk easily to the top of the obvious way running across the face of Harrison. Very rocky at first and with excellent views into the defile of Dungeon Ghyll it soon runs out into a whaleback of grassy fell with a line of cairns, and in front, the conical tower of Pike How.

Here the path begins to zig-zag down, until at a cairn the welcoming sight of the New Dungeon Ghyll may be seen, still far below! As the foot of Dungeon Ghyll itself is reached, there is a stile and a seat, then shortly afterwards the path running from the Old Dungeon Ghyll is found, where a left turn is made. It is now thankfully but a short distance to a welcoming bar and a well earned drink.

Walk 4: Blencathra

Distance: 4.8 miles (7.2km)

Height gained: 2400ft (732m)

Time: 3 to 5 hours.

Start: Threlkeld Car Park or discreet parking in the village. GR 319256.

Terrain: High rocky ridge with a little unavoidable easy scrambling (following the ridge in its entirety is a Grade 1 scramble) direct to Blencathra's summit. Easy return via the whole rim of the mountain, and the grassy slopes of Blease Fell. The route can be a serious undertaking under snow and ice often requiring full winter mountaineering equipment.

Maps: OS Landranger Sheet – 90 Penrith & Keswick (1:50 000).

Public transport: Buses run between Penrith and Keswick.

The Salutation Inn, Threlkeld; tel: (017687) 79614

The ancient, low, white painted Salutation Inn stands at the very foot of the hill with a fantastic view of the route from its small garden (look for the mural to the rear of the pub!). It is a welcoming pub, an outlet for Theakstons Ales, also serving good value food. Inside there is a stone-flagged area near the bar, and a carpeted one with a fireplace off to one side – most agreeable after a winter's walk! Children and dogs are made most welcome.

Blencathra

If I had to choose one mountain in the Lake District as a favourite, it would be Blencathra. It stands guard over the tiny village of Threlkeld like a partially clenched fist, with its three well-defined ridges reaching out to the valley floor. At each end are the broader expanses of Scales and Blease Fells, with Scales Fell hiding the serious ascent route of Sharp Edge. In between are the fingers of Doddick, Hall's and Gategill Fells with that of Hall's Fell offering the

The rim of Blencathra

most sporting (though not too serious) route, to the 2847ft (868m) summit. The ridges either side are easier, so may be used instead of Hall's, but do not have the satisfaction of aiming unerringly at the highest point.

The Walk

From the village leave the main street leftwards past the new industrial estate and go left again up the private road that is also signposted as a bridleway. Pass through the farmyard and the nearby gate – there is a seat here – to the weir at the foot of Gate Gill. Cross the stream and follow the well-trodden path onto the broad base of Hall's Fell; this climbs with pergatorial steepness up a worn trough in the peat. Odd patches of rock poke through the bracken as the way toils upwards. I have seen this track described as enchanting, but it is too steep and broad to hold too much interest. But better, far better, is to come.

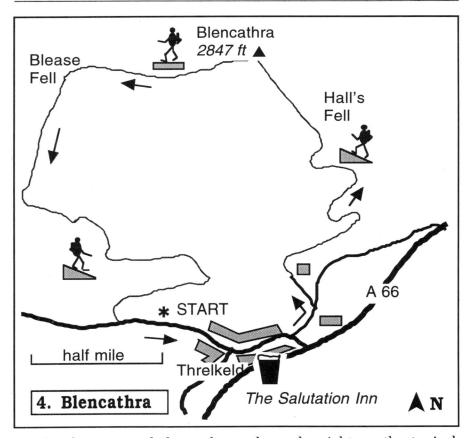

Blencathra
2847 ft ▲

Blease Fell

Hall's Fell

A 66

* START

half mile

Threlkeld

4. Blencathra

The Salutation Inn

▲ N

As height is gained the path trends to the right on the typical Northern Lakeland grey and spiky rock with views towards Penrith and the distant Pennines. At a cairn the view suddenly opens out, and Doddick and Scales Fells abruptly burst into view, and the path takes a straight line up the narrowing fell. The broader outlook is especially fine now, with Derwentwater and Catbells over the left shoulder, while behind is St John's in the Vale, with the great mass of the Eastern Fells forming both the immediate foreground and distant panorama. It starts getting more interesting from here. The drops into the depressions of Doddick and Gate Gill begin to converge and the increasingly rocky spine is compressed into what is known as Narrow Edge.

Easy scrambling leads to the first of the rock towers where a choice may be made. Either follow the ridge direct (a Grade 1 scramble, and only for the competent) or follow the well-trodden path as it weaves around the buttresses of grey rock. Some of these get close to the edge above big drops and, to make it all a little more exciting, even these involve a little easy scrambling where the path dies out. It crosses from side to side scrambling now and then across small slabs straight up the spine of the ridge. After a rocky tower the path crosses again to the left and winds its way to the summit trig point immediately ahead.

Virtually a mile of almost level walking along the top of the fell and the airy scrambling of the ridge is the reward for the toil. With an easy path it is possible to enjoy what must be one of the best views in England. From Cross Fell in the Pennines, right round to Skiddaw in the west, almost every major Lakeland mountain is in view with a few lakes glinting in the valleys to add a little spice to the scene. If, however, the cloud is down, the walk is almost like trekking along the top of a sea cliff with gentle slopes falling away to the north and the precipices of the deeply carved river valleys sensed away to the left.

All too soon, the path starts to fall away down the grass slopes of Blease Fell. This winds down steeply and disappears over a shoulder of fell on a cairned motorway. No real motorway has views like this though. This is the 'Back o' Skidda' and the views extend over Knott to the Scottish Hills and the Solway Firth. Odd patches of rock intrude then, the way begins to head back towards Threlkeld, again on a good, but steepening path.

Pass through a gate then follow the wall, crossing Blease Gill, then take the path on the right with a slate sign to Threlkeld. This follows the stream delightfully, to a wooden bridge and a seat, then out onto the road at a small green and the village car park. At Blease Road turn left, where just a few minutes' brisk walking bring you to the welcome sight of The Salutation with its stone flagged bar greeting all manner of weary feet.

Walk 5: A Crinkle Crags Traverse

Distance: 8 miles (12.8km)

Height gained: 2650ft (808m)

Time: 4 to 6 hours.

Start: Langdale Car Park near Old Dungeon Ghyll. GR 286061.

Terrain: Well marked paths to high and rugged ridge, one avoidable awkward section. Descent via easy to follow path.

Maps: OS Landranger Sheet 90 – Penrith & Keswick (1:50 000).

Public transport: Frequent buses run along Langdale.

The Old Dungeon Ghyll Hotel, Great Langdale; tel: (015394) 37272

The Old Dungeon Ghyll, or ODG as it is known to many walkers, is a climbers' hotel dating from the earliest days of the sport. It stands at the end of the road along Langdale, surrounded by some of the finest mountain scenery in Lakeland. It is a Free House serving a wide selection of ales and good food in a unique atmosphere – often there will be singers giving impromptu performances in the stone-flagged bar. It caters for all outdoor enthusiasts, and children and dogs are most welcome.

Crinkle Crags

Immediately behind the ODG is a line of crags guarding the lower reaches of the Langdale Pikes (see walk 3) and on the other side of the classic U-shaped valley rise the rugged heights of Crinkle Crags and Pike o' Blisco. It is a magnificent skyline, and once reached gives a mile of sublime high level walking as it twists and turns through crags and up and down outcrops. This walk starts easily as it approaches the Oxendale Valley before ascending between the Pike and the Crinkles high above Browney Gill.

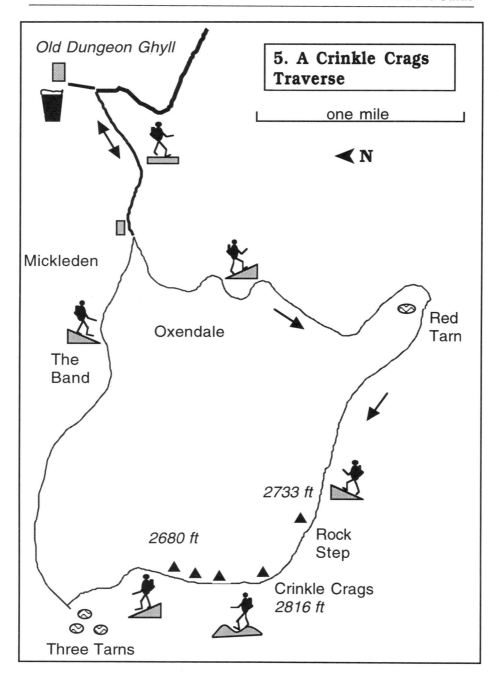

Old Dungeon Ghyll

5. A Crinkle Crags Traverse

one mile

◀ N

Mickleden

Oxendale

The
Band

Red
Tarn

2733 ft

2680 ft

Rock
Step

Crinkle Crags
2816 ft

Three Tarns

The Walk

Just after leaving the car park a small bridge is crossed onto the road. A right turn soon has the walk leaving the road at a sharp left-hand bend with a wooden signpost (Oxendale and the Band) to the still-surfaced farm track. Easy walking soon leads to the farm, the slopes of The Band rising just beyond, where arrows show the way to a gate and the start of a rougher track.

Soon after the gate the motorway of The Band leads off to the right – this is the way down in a few hours' time – but our route carries on through a kissing gate towards the valley bottom. Muddy at first, the way soon improves as a small brook runs alongside the path, and a couple more gates lead to the wide Oxendale Valley. The rocks scattered around the river are reminiscent of those found alongside Alpine streams, and give some idea of what the waters are like when in spate. Cross the wooden memorial footbridge and pick a way through the bleached boulders on the other side with the riven slopes of Crinkle Crags now immediately in front, the path rising towards the obvious col. The climb begins!

Some superfluous cairns (not the last unfortunately) mark the start of the climb as it leaves the stream bed, and a steep path ascends the open fellside. The going is good underfoot, with the way alternating between natural rock and a manufactured pathway of large well-set stones. Pausing on such steepness is all too easy, but in the case of this path the views really repay a quick breather. Those towards the confines of Hell Gill and the waterfall of Whorneyside Force are particularly fine. Ever upwards, crossing several small becks, the views just keep getting better. Crinkle Crags, the vast crag girt flanks of Bowfell and behind the whole sweep of the Langdale Pikes draws the eye. A landscape to be savoured.

A few short, manufactured zig-zags above Browney Gill bring a level section underfoot where the path can be plainly seen wandering away to the left before crossing to the right-hand side of the fell above the right-hand branch of the stream and Great Knott. The level section is short lived, the path soon reverts to its relentless angle, now over boulders until it drops into a stream bed just above a small

On Crinkle Crags ridge

waterfall. Climb out and continue to the junction just by Red Tarn. Here the path from Pike o' Blisco enters.

The next section leading off to the right is the least rewarding part of the whole route. The path toils across broad convex fells and the views are blotted out by nearby buttresses or by the very nature of the terrain. Fortunately this is short lived and a good view emerges of the Crinkle Crags ridge spreading out in front, with Bowfell, now appearing to be a continuation, beyond. A short, steep and stony pull then has the base of the first of the Crinkles reached. This is the start of one of the best miles in the whole of The Lake District.

This first Crinkle is a long ridge of bare rock traversed by scrambly paths before dropping into Great Cove. From here the second, and highest (2816ft, 858m) Crinkle rears up with the infamous 'Bad Step' blocking the way. Much has been written about this impasse in the logical ascent gully, and it seems to have gained a reputation more fearsome than it deserves. If you can climb a normal ladder then the ten-foot scramble should be within your capabilities; the holds are good and a couple of quick moves soon have the top within grasp. If the prospect of the short rock step is too daunting however, a way sneaks off to the left to reach the summit more easily.

The Scafell range is now centre stage as the path continues over the remaining tops. It ascends the cairned Crinkles by easy rocky paths and drops sometimes into small boggy hollows with the green fields of Langdale contrasting with the surrounding grey rocks. Soon the path descends for the final time, and the pass between Eskdale and Oxendale is reached at Three Tarns where a white stony track leads off rightwards and traverses the hillside. This is also a popular route to Bowfell, and the scoured buttresses of Bowfell Links are just above.

This stony path is the top section of The Band, and it leads directly to the farm at Stool End. On the way it winds along a broad ridge, sometimes level, sometimes descending quite steeply but always easy to follow as it is severely eroded, and is getting worse (please try to keep to the rocky path as venturing onto the grassy hillside worsens the problem). Soon, a wall and a wooden kissing gate are reached and the path now drops to the farm along the section viewed earlier. All that remains is to retrace your steps to the ODG and that welcome pint!

Walk 6: The Old Man and Dow

Distance: 8 miles (12.8km)

Height gained: 2875ft (877m)

Time: 5 to 7 hours.

Start: Coniston Car Park or in road near The Sun. GR 302976.

Terrain: Good paths over high fells, if the crest of Dow Crag is followed there is a certain degree of exposure and some simple scrambling. Easy escape routes exist on the route up The Old Man and from Goat's Hause, down to Goat's Water.

Maps: OS Landranger Sheet 96 – Barrow-in-Furness & South Lakeland area (1:50 000).

Public transport: Buses and ferries run to Coniston.

The Sun, Coniston; tel: (015394) 41248

The little village of Coniston nestles above the lake of the same name where so many water speed records were attempted. The Sun reflects this with Donald Campbell memorabilia in its cosy bar, it is attached to the hotel of the same name, built in 1902, and is just the sort of place to go after a day on the hill. An outlet for Old Man Ale, a ruby-coloured ale brewed in the village, as well as excellent food. Children and dogs welcome on the outside drinking area.

Coniston Old Man

Coniston Old Man is a popular excursion from Coniston village, especially as it is possible to 'cheat' by parking a good distance up the Walna Scar track – not so practical for the Pubhiker though! The top of Coniston Old Man is the culmination, and highest point, of a group of peaks known collectively as The Coniston Fells. The walk as described, however, climbs the Old Man by a popular, though interesting route, through the sometimes desolate scenery of The Coppermines Valley before taking an airy walk above the buttresses of Dow Crag – seen to such advantage from the top of the Old Man itself.

Descending the ridge from Dow Crag

The Walk

Assuming a start from the lane by The Sun, take the road alongside, which is signposted as a public footpath to Old Man and Levers Water. The road soon ends at a farm, where a gate on the left leads out to a track. This crosses a stream, then climbs above the tumbling Church Beck to where a bridge recrosses it. Ignore the bridge, and instead, continue up the now narrow path to a gate where the scene opens up to include the whole of the Coniston Fells. This is a scene of long-deserted industry, with spoil heaps and mine buildings scattered across the landscape, although they have now mellowed to blend in rather than impose.

Just after a sheepfold, the east face of the Old Man rears up in front and the easy-to-follow path leads unerringly towards the remains of the quarry. Continue climbing, now among the spoil heaps and ruins, up to the shattered remains of a cableway. The thick steel cables are still in place, along with the tumbledown buildings and the man-made ramp. It is difficult to imagine walking to work in these quarries, and the conditions that must have been endured during the winter by the workforce.

Just by a tunnel on the left and a fallen gantry, turn half-right and climb through the desolation. This is suddenly countered by Low Water bursting into view in a truly wild setting and it is this contrast between the quarry-wracked slopes and the natural splendours of the higher section of the mountain that make the route so interesting.

The way is obvious in front as the path zig-zags up to the left of the screes to join the ridge. Once the ridge is reached the views to the south burst out, with below, the length of Coniston Water stretching out towards the coastline of Morecambe Bay. All that remains is the pull to the summit (2633ft, 801m) just a few minutes slog away, where a huge cairn and wind shelter make an ideal place for a break. While on the summit it is worth casting an eye over the buttresses of Dow Crag, now completely dominating the scene, although the Scafell range try unsuccessfully to compete.

To eventually go south, the summit has to be quit in northwards, until a path can be picked up on the left leading down to the saddle between Coniston Old Man and Dow Crag. Rocky, this drops steeply on a rough path, losing over 500 precious feet (153m) in the process to Goat's Hause, where a descent may be made direct to Goat's Water, although this would miss the best part of the walk.

The path swings to the left, and regains 425 of those lost feet (130m) in about half a mile. It clings more or less to the crest of Dow Crag and follows a steep and rugged route through the rocks. The actual top of the fell can be avoided to the right on an intermittent path amongst boulders and grass, although the easy scramble required to attain the 2555ft (779m) summit is worthwhile. The ridge falls away in both directions, while immediately below is the awe-inspiring void of the actual crag.

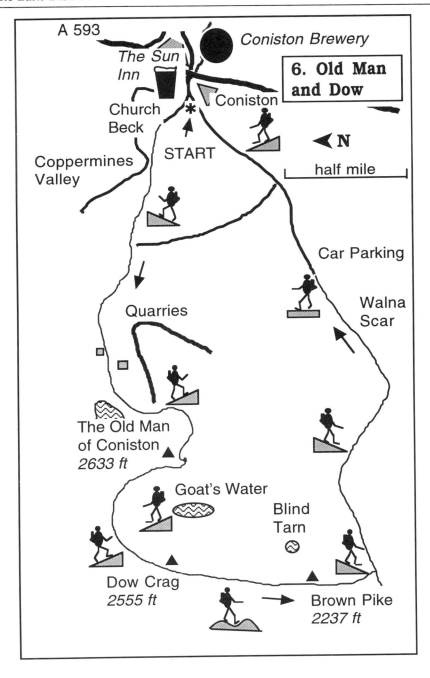

A 593

The Sun Inn

Coniston Brewery

6. Old Man and Dow

Church Beck

Coniston

START

◄ N

Coppermines Valley

half mile

Car Parking

Quarries

Walna Scar

The Old Man of Coniston
2633 ft

Goat's Water

Blind Tarn

Dow Crag
2555 ft

Brown Pike
2237 ft

From this airy perch the next objectives may be seen – first Buck Pike, then at the far end of the ridge Brown Pike. A good path that zig-zags down gently, traverses the first, then goes on to the rocky little summit of Brown Pike (2237ft, 682m) with its round wind shelter just to the left of the cairn. From here an easy path drops to the Walna Scar Road, just 242ft (74m) below – when the quarries were working this was a service road, although now it has no vehicular rights and is a bridleway.

Turn left onto this and wind downwards, passing some ruined buildings, then crossing the outflow from Goat's Water – Torver Beck – by Cove Bridge. Easy walking continues to the small car parking area mentioned earlier, where a gate leads onto a metalled road. This soon descends steeply, too steeply for aching legs and knees. The pain is quickly forgotten, however, as just past the old station yard the welcome sight of the Sun comes into view, closely followed by a glass of Old Man Ale.

Walk 7: The Fairfield Horseshoe

Distance: 10.5 miles (16.6km)

Height gained: 3532ft (1077m)

Time: 5 to 8 hours.

Start: Ambleside Car Park. GR 374047.

Terrain: Good paths over high fells, some grassy, some stony. Route finding can be awkward in mist on Fairfield itself, otherwise there should be no navigational problems. It is basically up one side and down the other! It is, however, a long and serious walk that may require all the daylight of a short winter's day.

Maps: OS Landranger Sheet 90 – Penrith & Keswick (1:50 000).

Public transport: Plenty of buses pass through Ambleside.

The White Lion Hotel, Ambleside; tel: (015394) 33140

The parking in Ambleside can be very difficult, so the best place to start the walk is the main car park just down the road (this can get very crowded in season), leaving the pub for later. The White Lion is a big hotel with large public bars on the ground floor. Bass is on hand-pump and good food is served – watch for the daily specials. Children and dogs are welcome and being a hotel, comfortable accommodation is available.

The Fairfield Horseshoe

The Fairfield Horseshoe is one of Lakeland's classic walks and I make no apologies for including it here. It really is that good! The whole route is long and over high fells, and has a certain feeling of remoteness, while the views from Fairfield itself are superb. It takes in 8 separate fells (as defined in Wainwright's Eastern Fells) starting with Low Pike, and ending several airy miles later with a descent of Nab Scar. In between, the walking is on lofty rounded ridges, the ascent being alongside one of the most amazing dry-stone walls to be found anywhere, and the pinnacle is Fairfield itself at 2863ft (873m).

The Walk

From the car park, take the road opposite (Smithy Brow), passing the Golden Rule – see walk 1 – on the way, and continue until Sweden Bridge Lane is reached on the left. As the path climbs there are fine views back over Ambleside, towards the Coniston Fells and the Langdale Pikes; these set the theme for the rest of the walk. At a gate the road is quit and the way becomes stony underfoot – tarmac is not to be felt again for getting on for 9 miles – and the walk proper starts! As the path climbs, the first glimpses of The Horseshoe stretching out in front coincide with the increasing babble of Scandale Beck on the left. Just by some attractive cascades the path drops slightly to the narrow arch of High Sweden Bridge – from here until the return to the valley, the walking is all on open fells.

Cross the stream and double back briefly to follow a small watercourse as it flows to join Scandale Beck. A well-worn path leads to a ladder stile where a continuation of the path strikes up the hillside. At a stile crossing the wall to the left a path comes up from Low Sweden Bridge. This is attained by the lane just before the Golden Rule, and is a shorter, though less pleasant route. This path may, however, be followed rightwards to avoid the awkward rock step of the upper path. Keep climbing however, to the wall running along the fell ridge. This is steep, but the height has to be gained sometime so it may as well be now! At the wall turn right and follow the path to the rock step, which may be easily surmounted to gain the top of a small buttress.

The views just keep getting better, although the path underfoot does not, becoming boggy in places. The wetness is soon left and, just in front, beyond a few low crags, is the proud little peak of Low Pike (1657ft, 505m) already seeming high above Windermere. When this is attained, the wall is still there running across the fell-top and on to the next objective High Pike (2155ft, 657m). The ascent to this

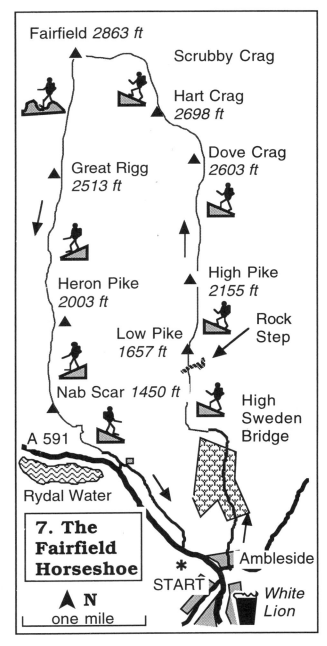

Fairfield 2863 ft

Scrubby Crag

Hart Crag 2698 ft

Dove Crag 2603 ft

Great Rigg 2513 ft

Heron Pike 2003 ft

High Pike 2155 ft

Low Pike 1657 ft

Rock Step

Nab Scar 1450 ft

High Sweden Bridge

A 591

Rydal Water

7. The Fairfield Horseshoe

▲ N

one mile

START

Ambleside

White Lion

is steep, gaining 600ft (183m) in just over half a mile, and yes, it follows the wall all the way to the cairn.

The next objective is Dove Crag at 2603ft (793m), and again the path is defined by the presence of the wall, making navigation absolutely foolproof. The down-side of the easy navigation is the comparative paucity of views, and many walkers will feel that they would wish to leave the wall behind. However, once on the summit's rocky platform a tremendous panorama opens out with Fairfield dominating the northern aspect. More immediate, however, is the 2698ft (822m) summit of Hart Crag.

Although this is just 95ft (29m) higher, the path has to suffer 350ft (107m) of ascent, again following the wall to the flattish ridge that forms the top of the fell. This is it! The wall ends and the views are unsullied by grey rocks. What views too. To the west stand most of Lakeland's most prominent fells, from Crinkle Crags and Harrison Stickle via the Scafells to Great Gable and Pillar; while blocking much of the view to the north-west, stands the final peak in the ascent, Fairfield.

Just one mile and a little over 300ft (91m) of ascent remain to the jewel in this particular crown. First, above Scrubby Crag, then the other cliffs guarding the end of Deepdale, the path ascends gently across the domed top of the fell. In mist, the 2863ft (873m) summit can be a confusing place and the northern band of crags can make it a dangerous one too. On a good day however, the effort of getting there is rewarded with a breathtaking view, especially to the north, where the panorama of mountains has been hidden by the bulk of the fell itself. The eye is drawn to the line of hills from Dollywaggon Pike, over Helvellyn and on to distant Blencathra just peeping into the picture. It could have been designed with photographs in mind!

From Fairfield it is all 'down hill' although the first mile of descent still manages to contain 140ft (43m) of ascent. Almost due south across the stony, then grassy expanse is Great Rigg (2513ft, 766m), a rounded whale-back of a hill and the first nail in the return journey. A good path gives speedy walking high above Dunmail Raise to the right, and the deep valley of Rydal Beck, with the eastern sweep of the Horseshoe to the left. Follow the cairns southwards to the steepening leading towards Heron Pike. This, at 2003ft is the final major height of the round, and is a final grassy bastion of the high fells. It really is downhill from now.

At an old wall, the path continues alongside it to the final rocky outcrop of Nab Scar (1450ft, 442m) overlooking Grasmere. From here, the descent is a knee-crunching series of loose and shaly twists and turns. I always think that after such a stupendous high level walk, Nab Scar is a scruffy and worn finale. By now, even the views – less impressive from these lower heights – have began to wane and tiredness is detracting from most other senses just leaving the aching legs! I am always glad to get off Nab Scar.

The track soon returns to the valley by Rydal Mount, and follows the metalled road off to the left. This is signposted to the Rambler's Teashop – set just on the edge of the tumbling Rydal Beck – and passes through the cluster of buildings before emerging onto the park drive. Easy walking among fine mature trees soon has the way crossing Scandale Beck, and veering rightwards to join the A591 at a set of ornamental gates. Ambleside is just a few minutes' walk away, and following Rydal Road to Market Place soon has the comfort of the White Lion Hotel to hand.

Helvellyn from Fairfield

The Monsal Viaduct

The Peak District

The Peak district is the most popular of all England's National Parks. Surrounded as it is by large industrial cities it has a significant proportion of the country's population on its doorstep. Comprising about 550 square miles, it may be divided into two main areas; the gritstone Dark Peak of the north, and the gentler White Peak, with its lush, limestone Dales to the south.

The walks in this section cover both areas, with those on the high plateau of Kinder Scout being the most serious (see walks 13 and 14). Here walkers are almost certain to encounter the fast flying grouse on the heather and bracken covered slopes, while in winter, they may be lucky enough to see a mountain hare in its white winter coat. It is in winter that these inhospitable uplands should not be underestimated, the weather can at times be Arctic, and the broad tops of these hills can easily confound navigation.

To the south lie the gentler Derbyshire Dales, a high dome of limestone cut by deep, often craggy gorges. Criss-crossed by dry stone walls and with white stone villages nestling amid the green hills, it is hard to imagine this is the same county. The walking here is generally on easier paths, often signposted, and as an extra bonus for the 'Pubhiker', typically visiting several charming villages (with pubs of course) en-route.

A further feature of the area is the almost unbroken fault that gives the Eastern Gritstone Edges. These are visited by route No. 9, and give easier walking on good paths, but in the sterner landscape of the millstone grit. Many of these edges were quarried, and the walker will often come across part finished mill-stones, still lying where they were discarded when the industry collapsed.

For the walker and real ale enthusiast the Peak District is ideal; the area has a good spread of pubs, and it is rare to find one that does not serve the live product. Most of the pubs tend to dispense, as expected, Midlands and Northern beers; some, such as the rather strong Robinson's Old Tom are especially worth seeking out. Derbyshire is also blessed with half a dozen breweries of its own, with the village of Fenny Bentley boasting two micros, one of which, Leather-Britches, also has as a sideline: their own beer sausages.

To follow the seven routes in this section these maps are recommended: OS Landranger sheets 110 and 119 (1:50 000).

Walk 8: Black Rock

Distance: 8 miles (12.8km)

Height gained: 755ft (230m)

Time: 3 to 4 hours.

Start: Whatstandwell car park, GR 332544 (alternative start at GR 300570)

Terrain: Varied paths through farmland some canal towpath, climb to high rock outcrop.

Maps: OS Landranger Sheet 119 – Buxton, Matlock and Dove Dale (1:50 000).

Public transport: BR at Whatstandwell and Cromford, Buses including the TransPeak run along A6.

Derwent Hotel, Whatstandwell; tel: (01773) 856616

Situated just by a sharp bend on the A6 and right next to the river whose name it bears, the Derwent Hotel is a large and imposing building in the dark gritstone of the area. Close to bus stop and station, and with a public car park nearby it makes for an ideal 'pub-walk'. Within its thick walls it is a quiet haven serving Kimberley beers and a good selection of food lunchtime and evening. Children welcome, but dogs in bars only when food is not being served – there is though, an extensive garden.

Black Rock

The gaunt, wind eroded heights of Black Rock (951ft, 322m) are impressively situated above the village of Cromford, and are reached via some excellent and little used paths. The old, now disused High Peak railway line which passes the limestone screes at the foot of the rocks, and the towpath of the 18th century Cromford Canal – with the added interest of the steam powered Leawood pumping station – give extra impetus to the walk.

The Walk

Starting at the pub, or the small car park at the end of the now disused Cromford Canal walk briefly along the road, past the pub and across the river. The parallel road, railway, canal and river are said to be the closest to each other at this point than at any other site in Britain, although the A6 nowadays carries by far the heaviest traffic. Just around the bend, follow the road signposted to Alderwasley, and after a few minutes the footpath on the right.

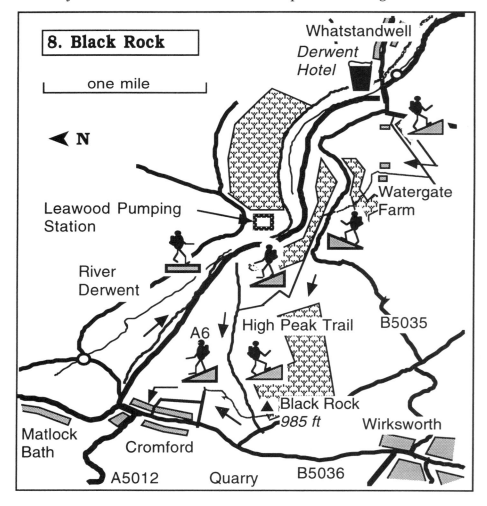

8. Black Rock

one mile

◄ N

Whatstandwell
*Derwent
Hotel*

Watergate Farm

Leawood Pumping Station

River Derwent

A6

High Peak Trail

B5035

Black Rock
985 ft

Wirksworth

Matlock Bath

Cromford

A5012

Quarry

B5036

Climb straight at first, to an easily missed left turn scaling a steep bank. At the top, cross a drive and walk gently uphill on a well-marked path across meadows. About ten minutes walking brings a path crossing where the route turns right, downhill.

At the foot of the hill, cross a couple of stiles to Watergate Farm where the route is channelled between a pair of walls, with a lake to the left. After a stile the way climbs steeply alongside a wall to a squeeze stile. This is definitely one to watch the footing on if painful and embarrassing impalement is to be avoided. A gravel track and a grassy rake lead past a farm, where an incredibly vocal, but fortunately tethered, dog will get your heart beating even if the slope does not. After the farm the path levels out and passes into an area of woodland before dropping to a field via a series of rucksack snagging squeezes.

Cross the road and take the gravel surfaced bridleway opposite, which gives easy walking for about a mile before dropping to join the High Peak Trail (the former railway line), where the junction is marked by a long abandoned quarry. The long uphill grind, passing lichenous gritstone outcrops, is bound to make you wonder as to the wisdom of building a railway here in the first place, even more so when you pass the winding house at the summit. A steam engine was housed here to pull loaded trains up the incline, it being far too steep for a friction driven railway engine to manage. The fine views, and convenient benches make this a good place to rest awhile.

The path suddenly becomes flat, and easy walking soon leads to the car park and picnic area at Black Rock. Just near the car park, a path branches off to the left and, after a few trees, emerges onto the scree at the foot of the rocks. Although Black Rock is wind-eroded Ashover Grit, the scree is limestone, contrasting sharply with the dark, and sometimes brooding towers.

At the top of the screes, a way may be found onto the sloping summit of the rocks, which at around 1000ft (322m) commands a fine view up the Derwent Valley and the limestone gorge of Matlock Bath. The gritstone walls fall away near vertically for eighty feet (25m) or so to the north, and this is the preserve of the rock-climber, no walker's routes here! To descend, simply retrace your steps over the easier back of the crag and return to the screes and then the Trail.

At the top of Black Rock

Turn right, and after a few minutes take the footpath signposted to Cromford. A couple of squeeze stiles, and it is all downhill. Pass some rocky outcrops and take the farm track which leads out into the top of the village. Small lanes and a footpath emerge onto the main village street at Bedehouse Lane. Turn right, past the pub (perhaps!) and continue down the hill possibly treating yourself to one of Arkwrights Store's superb ice creams.

At the A6, cross over, turn right and take the road on the left to the mill and the Cromford Canal. This starts as a narrow stream running beneath beetling limestone crags, and is fed with water from the soughs of the old lead mines, before opening out into the canal proper at the cluster of buildings that were Cromford Wharf. The towpath of the canal is to form the final section of the walk.

Although flat, this is anything but boring. In a short distance High Peak Junction is reached where the railway and the canal met, then there is Leawood pumping station where a steam driven pump draws water from the River Derwent far below and spits great gobs of it out into the canal. This is in steam on selected Sundays throughout the year, and is definitely worth a visit as it is possible to walk high among the machinery and the huge rocking beam.

A high aqueduct carries the canal above the river, and the path crosses to the opposite bank to wind through a long dark tunnel. All that remains is to follow the towpath, keeping a watchful eye open for the multitude of wildlife (it is now a nature reserve) including, hovering almost motionless in the clear water, as many pike as I have seen anywhere. Plentiful water birds are an added attraction, and it is rare for the patient watcher to not see a flash of amethyst as a kingfisher darts off downstream. All too soon the end is reached, and it is back to the car park, bus stop and railway station. Oh, and the Derwent Hotel!

Walk 9: The Eastern Gritstone Edges

Distance: 7.5 miles (12km)

Height gained: 1030ft (314m)

Time: 4 hours.

Start: OS Ref 280722.

Terrain: Tracks and paths along gritstone edges, generally good, one avoidable awkward section.

Maps: OS Landranger Sheet 119 – Buxton, Matlock and Dove Dale (1:50 000).

Public transport: Buses along A619.

The Robin Hood Inn, Baslow, just off A619; tel: (01246) 583186

The Robin Hood is the local pub for walkers, climbers and golfers taking their sport on the area's moorland delights. An attractive stone building with the golf course behind, it is also handy for the Eric Byne campsite and is a good starting point for this interesting circular walk. There are good views of Birchen Edge from the Climbers' Bar and the small garden. The beers are Mansfield's celebrated ales and food is available lunchtime and evenings. Children and dogs are welcome.

The Eastern Edges

The gritstone of the Peak District forms outcrops almost continuously down the eastern side of the Park, following a huge natural fault line. These are the edges so beloved of rock climbers, formed from a unique form of hard sandstone. Many of the edges were quarried in the past to form grind-stones, an industry killed by the introduction of manufactured carborundum. Birchen Edge stands at about the 1000ft contour, and is crowned by Nelson's Monument, while high above Barr Brook is a similar monolith erected in Wellington's memory. Here also is the intriguing Eagle Stone, the ascent of which used to be a local test piece for young men wishing to marry.

The Walk

From the pub, or adjoining public car park, head briefly uphill on the B6050 to a ladder stile, cross over, and follow the broad sandy path towards the monument-crowned edge. Easy walking, gently uphill through bracken and small trees soon leads to a fork in the track. Take the right-hand option, and follow this, steeper now as it narrows and winds its way over occasional boulders, to end abruptly at Birchen Edge.

Popular with rock-climbers (most of the climbs have names relating to Nelson), the crag still has plenty of breaches to allow the walker to its windy top. One of these is almost immediately beneath the monument and is the climber's easy way down, this gives a short scrambly section to the top (easier ways may be found further on). The actual monolith makes a fine viewpoint,

Nelson's monument

with the Derwent Valley stretching away into the distance and the far hills providing a purple backdrop. The three massive boulders just beyond continue the nautical theme, and have the names of Victory, Reliance and Royal Soverin [sic] carved into them.

Perhaps reflecting on whether to become a climber, follow the good path along the Edge to the end of the crag. Here, by the trig point, the path drops to the open moorland and continues to a stile leading onto the B6050. Go straight across the junction and turn left at the surfaced track just beyond Bar Brook. Fifteen minutes' easy walking brings Wellington's Monument (another superb viewpoint) to hand. An excellent spot for a rest.

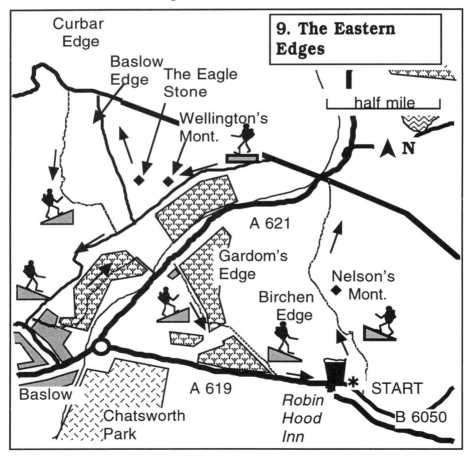

Follow the track off to the right past the Eagle Stone; the ascent of this, before becoming sport for rock-climbers at the beginning of the century, was said to be a test piece for men wishing to marry local girls. Getting up is difficult enough, getting down again – well! Leaving the stone in peace, continue along the path. Soon the ramparts of Curbar Edge come into view, and the road is reached at Curbar Gap. Turn left, on the path above the road to a footpath also to the left. This leads pleasantly to a junction with a bridleway and a gate in the wall, opening out onto the slopes below Baslow Edge.

Walk, now parallel to the crags to a meeting of paths, take the left-hand fork, and plod uphill through the strange rounded mounds and onto the path running along the scarp edge. Left will take you back to Wellington's Monument – and a short-cut; right, however, will bring you via Baslow Bar to one of the Peak's most secret paths. Just after passing the Lady Wall Well, at Moor Cottage, a small road and a stile leads into woodland. Take first the right fork, then the left, slightly uphill and deeper into the trees.

For about a mile, the almost overgrown path contours the hillside high above the speeding traffic on the A621. Although not shown on the map there are several small streams and their attendant boggy areas to cross, and at one point huge moss-covered boulders block the path. At some points a machete seems quite desirable, then, at an old wall the character changes, and the path dips briefly into dark coniferous woodland before emerging into the light again at a stile.

With the monument plainly visible above (the short-cut rejoins here), turn downhill and cross the peat-stained brook via a small wooden bridge before climbing to the road. Turn left onto the footpath until opposite Cupola Cottage, then cross to the gap in the wall by the cottage. Make the most of the flat going; the path soon climbs, picking its way through boulders and trees, to a fine panorama at the top.

Descend now, passing Moorside Rocks, an isolated outcrop of rounded gritstone which repays the easy scramble to its top, and follow the well-trodden path back to the road, where after a stile, a couple of left turns soon brings the welcome sight of the Robin Hood. Now you can feel you have earned that beer in the Climbers' Bar.

Walk 10: Monsal Dale and the Magpie Mine

Distance: 13 miles (21km)

Height gained: 820ft (250m)

Time: 5 to 6 hours.

Start: Monsal Trail Car Park. GR 223689.

Terrain: Easy paths and tracks.

Maps: OS Landranger Sheet 119 – Buxton, Matlock and Dove Dale (1:50 000).

Public transport: Frequent buses run along A6.

The Packhorse Inn, Little Longstone; tel: (01629) 640471

Little Longstone's tiny stone-built Packhorse Inn is a delight. A pub since 1787, it welcomes walkers to its traditional tap room and small enclosed garden. Ales from Marston's are served, as is good food, and children are welcomed in the bar providing food is ordered. Dogs may be taken into the small, enclosed garden. Plenty of other pubs are to be found in the walk's thirteen miles, so it could take several hours longer than expected!

Limestone and Lead Mines

Monsal Head, with its fabulous views, is one of the 'honey pot' locations of the Peak District. Quite rightly too! This walk gets away from the crowds by following the River Wye and then Deep Dale to visit the gaunt remains of Magpie Mine, a long disused lead mine, and now a field study centre. It then descends to the River Wye, via the intriguing Black Marble mines in Little Shacklow Wood, before going on to the picture postcard village of Ashford-in-the-Water. The

The Packhorse Inn

river then provides a fine return to Bakewell, home of the famous puddings. Oh, and even more pubs!

The Walk

The station at Bakewell provides a fine start to this walk. Forget, however, about timetables and parking problems, this is long disused, and now forms the start of the Monsal Trail. Pass to the left of the station buildings, and follow the gravel track-bed northwards. Easy walking alongside banks where wild raspberries grow in profusion soon brings you to a station (now a house). Shortly after this a path crosses the line, and this is followed to the right.

Grassy tracks and a series of stiles soon lead to the road, and a left turn, in Little Longstone – just alongside the walled garden of a farm. As well as the pub, the remainder of the village is a delight. Tiny cottage gardens, a blaze of colour in summer, lead down to the road from pretty stone houses huddled together against the winter weather that can buffet these heights. All this, means that the short distance along the road from the Packhorse to Monsal Head passes quickly.

At Monsal Head is another pub (surely too soon to stop again!), tea rooms and definitely not man-made (well not all of it anyway) a fantastic view along the River Wye towards Miller's Dale. Just below is a distinctly human element in the landscape, in the shape of the many-arched viaduct that carries the continuation of our recently-quit railway line after it emerges from a tunnel. If the line were open today what a draw it would be! Our route, however, drops to the river bank beyond and far below.

At a gap in the wall, a well made path leads down to the left. With a fence on the 'steep side' this drops steadily towards the river – soon to make its presence known by the rumble from the weir – and out into the broad base of the dale. As the footbridge is approached, on the left, is the huge landslip of Fin Cop. Also known as Hob's House where the surface limestone has slipped downhill on a thin layer of lava leaving the distinctive 'houses' up to thirty feet (10m) high.

Cross the bridge and turn left, although the banks by the weir

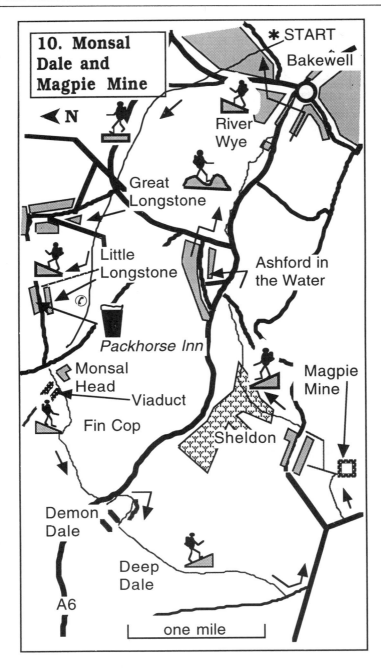

10. Monsal Dale and Magpie Mine

N

START
Bakewell

River Wye

Great Longstone

Little Longstone

Packhorse Inn

Ashford in the Water

Monsal Head

Viaduct

Fin Cop

Magpie Mine

Sheldon

Demon Dale

Deep Dale

A6

one mile

make a fine sheltered spot for a break, and follow the obvious broad path alongside the river. This is the domain of the trout, and their shadowy shapes may often be seen as they rise to catch flies (although it seems, rarely those with a hook in them!), little black and white dippers may also be frequently seen as they bob about on the midstream rocks.

Just after Brushfield Hough a signpost points towards White Lodge, and a short boggy area then a wall stile brings the route out onto the A6. Cross with care, and walk up through the picnic area and over a stile. A path now climbs gradually towards the foot of Demon Dale. There is no legal access to this short but interesting dale, although there is plenty of evidence of walkers using it. Here therefore, the actual right of way goes left, then at a sign for Deep Dale right again, beneath towers of crumbling rock and between gnarled trees to drop into Deep Dale just above Demon Dale.

Although steadily uphill, the next section is easy, following the wall. First on one side, then, just after some workings, on the other, until the farm track is reached as the dale levels out. There are many options here, although for the best views of Magpie Mine it is best to continue to the road and turn left. In half a mile a bend is reached; carry straight on towards Monyash and in a few more metres take the stile over the wall. Across the fields are the remains of the mine buildings, a wild and inhospitable workplace.

The area around the buildings (now a study centre, where a leaflet may be bought giving information about the mine) repays a little exploration. Especially interesting is the 728 feet (222m) deep shaft beneath the winding gear, which always exhibits a draught from the drainage sough in the Wye Valley. On a stormy day, the ruins give the visitor an insight into how hard life must have been for the late 19th century lead miner.

Leave the mine on the footpath to Sheldon, then turn right towards Ashford, crossing a multitude of dry stone walls en-route to the road. Turn right, then at Lower Farm left onto the path descending steeply towards the wood – note the sign warning of mine-shafts! After a gate, height is lost rapidly as the path dives into the wood, passing the now overgrown walls that are all that remains of the long deserted Black Marble workings. As the woodland begins to thin out, a wider track curves to the right and leads to the river. By turning left here, it is possible to reach the outflow of the Magpie Sough which drained the workings of the mine. Right, however, leads downstream, and back towards Bakewell.

Just ten minutes or so leads onto a minor road by a weir, this is followed down to the A6, and after a further couple of minutes to Ashford. A delightful stone-built village with an ancient sheep-wash bridge; there are plenty of opportunities for refreshment and places to take a rest, perhaps even feed the ducks!

Continue through the village and take the old road past the mill and over the river. At the main road a footpath is taken into the riverside meadows which give good, although surprisingly undulating walking for a mile or so to a cluster of houses. Follow the footpath through these and out into fields again, and all too soon back onto the A6. All that remains is to turn left and follow the pavement back into Bakewell. A final sting in the tail remains however, as after crossing the river for the final time, the steep roads leading back to the car park can be almost too much for tired legs.

Walk 11: Cown Edge and Lantern Pike

Distance: 8.5 miles (13.5km)

Height gained: 850ft (260m)

Time: 4 to 5 hours.

Start: Rowarth public car park, OS Ref 010890 (alternative start, off-road parking on Monk's Road at GR 020924)

Terrain: Tracks and paths, generally good.

Maps: OS Landranger Sheet 110 – Sheffield and Huddersfield area (1:50 000).

Public transport: Buses run along A624, BR in Glossop.

Little Mill Inn, Rowarth; tel: (01663) 743178

The Little Mill Inn is a rambling gritstone building pleasantly situated next to a stream, and has plenty of outdoor seating – some of which features a water-wheel alongside – and more unusually a railway carriage. It is a Free House serving a variety of real ales and good food, which also offers accommodation. Children and dogs are made most welcome. For this walk it may be visited half-way by using the alternative start.

Cown Edge

Cown Edge is the final defiant outpost of rough moorland before Greater Manchester forces the wild places into submission, and it forms the basis of a fine round walk which also visits Lantern Pike. Although only of modest height (1177ft -359m) the Pike commands fine views over Kinder Scout and, to the south-west, the hills surrounding the Vale of Goyt. The route remains fairly dry at all times so is a good choice for when the higher moors are likely to be too wet, or you just don't want to scrub the boots again!

The Little Mill

The Walk

Just opposite the pub a road – declared unfit for motors – leads uphill between farms, soon becoming steep and rocky, grinding upwards within steep vegetated banks and over tilted slabs of gritstone. As it begins to level, so the views improve and the enjoyment suddenly becomes more apparent!

After the toil, an easy mile or so leads down past Wethercotes Farm to the minor road high above the Sett Valley; the farm seems to be populated entirely by manic dogs whose chains stop them just short of a mouthful of leg. With body intact, but nerves a little shattered, turn left onto the road, and in a couple of hundred metres left again onto a bridleway ascending gradually towards Lantern Pike. After about ten minutes an eroded track forks leftwards alongside a wall where a gate is next to the National Trust sign leads to a narrow path clinging tightly to another wall to the ridge of the Pike.

Ten minutes very pleasant walking with superb views across Kinder bring the Royce Topograph to hand. Dedicated to Edwin

Royce for his work in "securing the freedom of the hills", it shows an outline sketch of the skyline with distances to many surrounding features, and is a peaceful place when shared only with the grouse. Eventual descent is made via the eroded north ridge to rejoin the bridleway at another NT signpost.

Passing through the gate the way goes half-left until a multiple finger post indicates the route via Matley Moor. An effortless saunter along a flat stony lane between walls passes Matleymoor Farm to follow the footpath westwards where the scarp of Cown Edge Rocks forms the skyline. A surfaced road is crossed to where a lofty stile, almost qualifying as a scramble, gives access to a field. This is crossed to the far right-hand corner, where another stile is found beneath a tree, and a track leading down to Cloughead Farm.

Beyond the farm a small wooden bridge and a stile bring a good narrow path up a steep field underfoot. At a gap in the wall head for Far Cown Edge Farm, where, after a short muddy section next to the buildings, a metalled track leads to another crossing it. Walk leftwards for a short distance and take the sign-posted footpath parallel to the ridge until Rocks Farm is reached. Here, turn briefly left to find another footpath sign pointing across a rough field crisscrossed by sheep tracks. The right of way, however, goes straight across to meet the Monk's Road a short distance from Sitch Farm. Here, you turn left and a few minutes of brisk walking up the road leads to a small car parking area (a good alternative start point).

From the parking area follow the road westwards for a short distance before taking the footpath between the wall and fence towards Cown Edge Rocks. After a stretch of sunken path, the narrow track skirts the impressive coombe formed by the shattered rocks, giving fine views down into the landslipped arena and the distinctive ridge of the Mare's Back below. Crossing a stile on a narrow neck of land between a plantation and the rocks, the route leads gently downhill to a path crossing.

The wall and fence are followed leftwards to one stile, then another in the top left corner of the field, where the views over the other hills begin to open out. Through a gate and gently upwards between rough pastures, until a large spiral stile on the crest leads

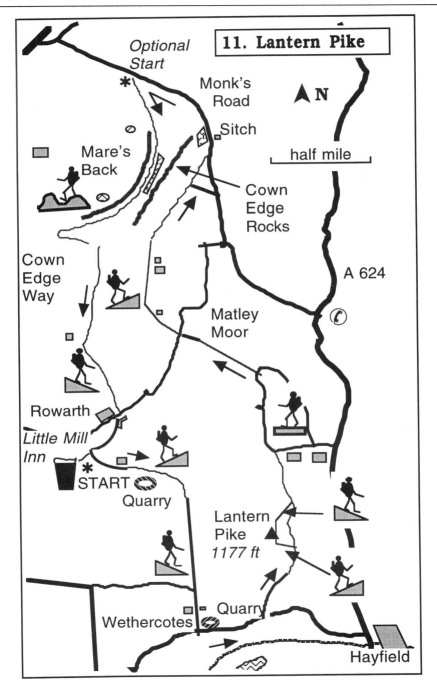

11. Lantern Pike

Optional Start

Monk's Road

Sitch

N

half mile

Cown Edge Rocks

Mare's Back

Cown Edge Way

A 624

Matley Moor

Rowarth

Little Mill Inn

START

Quarry

Lantern Pike 1177 ft

Wethercotes

Quarry

Hayfield

out into the field on the right. Upon crossing the field a wide grassy path is met leading towards a wall on the near skyline with the distant hills beyond.

Striding along the path, it is worth remembering that the true right of way descends to Near Slack, although the described route is obviously well trodden. As the path nears a broken dry stone wall it drops into a depression and parallels the fence for about 100 metres to another stile. After the stile the path heads for the edge through a landscape of tussocky grass and gorse to drop steeply towards Rowarth, where after a stone squeeze-stile the path runs between the houses and onto the road.

After a few more metres turn left at a large 18th century dwelling to descend the bridleway past 'The White House'. Increasingly rocky, this is followed to the level of the river and back to the pub, and a warm welcome in summer or winter.

Walk 12: Cave Dale and the Great Ridge

Distance: 8 miles (12.8km)

Height gained: 1447ft (441m)

Time: 4 to 5 hours.

Start: Castleton car park. GR 149830

Terrain: Limestone dale and high ridge, strenuous. The ridge can be very exposed to bad weather.

Maps: OS Landranger Sheet 110 – Sheffield and Huddersfield area (1:50 000).

Public transport: BR at Hope & Edale, buses run through Castleton.

The Castle, Castleton; tel: (01433) 620578

Standing on a prominent corner plot in the popular village of Castleton, The Castle, serving Stone's ales, is ideally situated for this walk. It is warm and cozy in winter and has plenty of outside seating for the finer months, all overlooked by the imposing remains of William Peveril's Norman castle – which is well worth a visit. Children and dogs are welcome, the latter only when food is not being served however. The village with its show caves and shops selling Blue John jewellery has something for everyone, and it may seem difficult to tear oneself away for a walk – but it's worth it.

The Great Ridge

The limestone of the White Peak ends abruptly, separated from the northern moors by a band of Edale Shale. This outcropping forms one of the finest walks in the Peak District. Stretching two miles from Mam Tor (1696ft, 517m) in the west to Lose Hill at 1561ft (476m), it provides a glorious walkway, never dropping below about

At the summit of Mam Tor

1300ft (396m), with the Vale of Edale and Kinder Scout on the left. This area can be rather crowded – although the bulk of humanity is left behind at Mam Tor. This is the grandly-named Great Ridge, and is the only walk of its type in the Peak District. It can, however, be a bleak and inhospitable one in winter, when it is necessary to be well equipped.

The Walk

The best place to start this walk is from the pay and display car park in the centre of Castleton as, on summer weekends, parking in this tiny village is at a premium. From here take the road almost immediately opposite – Castle Street – and follow this past the chosen pub and the church, then turning left, past the small triangular green on to Dale Cottage. Here a sign points the way to Cave Dale and the Limestone Way.

   At the end of the cottages, the walk proper begins at a gate where the crags bear in on either side and the path becomes polished limestone. It winds upwards among outcrops and ridges of rock, many of which have caves at their foot. As it becomes steeper there is a fine view behind of the keep of the castle balanced above the void, and the path leads through another narrowing to a gate.

From here the valley opens out to become U-shaped with the path following an old wall, stony at first it soon becomes grassy as it leaves the crowds below. Easy walking soon leads to another steepening, where a gate leads through the wall at a map. After the uphill of the dale, the level walking on firm grass is an easy way to consume some distance, and in no time at all the obvious path leads to a pair of gates, and a stile leading out onto the farm track.

Turn right here, and follow the track pleasantly, round a bend, and on past Rowter Farm; where it becomes surfaced. A few minutes more brings the track out to the B6061, where a footpath is seen crossing the wall almost opposite. This leads easily, with the bulk of Mam Tor ahead, past the depression and caves of Windy Knoll where the bones of mammoth and wolves have been found, though now it is a fine sheltered place to stop for a rest.

After Windy Knoll, the meat of the route starts at a double stile leading onto the slopes of Mam Tor, the 'Shivering Mountain'. Nowadays, a gritstone stairway leads up the hill (necessary to absorb the damaging impact of the thousands of visitors the peak receives yearly), and the top, with its fine outlook is soon reached. One of the best views, however, is along the two miles of the Great Ridge, the undulating whaleback linking our present hill with Lose Hill, and which forms the next part of the walk. One of the finest in the Peak!

Almost as soon as the heights of Mam Tor are left, the crowds thin out, and the ridge is the preserve of the more enthusiastic of walkers. A superb and airy promenade soon leads gently down to the pass of Hollins Cross, where a short cut may be made straight down to Castleton; this, however, misses the next, and to my mind the best hill of the ridge – Back Tor. Made of the same shales as Mam Tor, it is not as high and, being further from the road, its rocky top can often be a haven of quiet at the busiest times.

The path climbs gradually from Hollins Cross, until a stile just

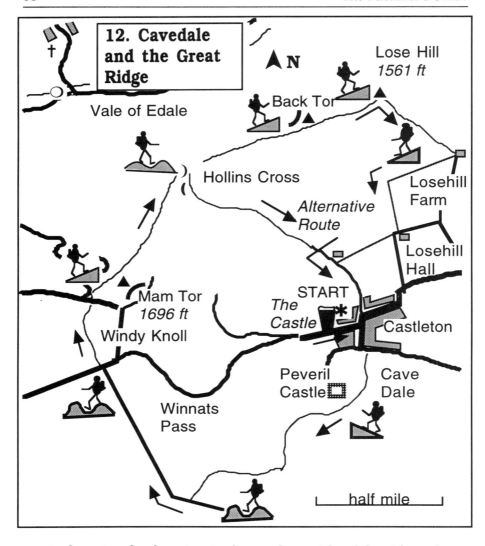

12. Cavedale and the Great Ridge

▲ N

Vale of Edale

Lose Hill
1561 ft

Back Tor

Hollins Cross

Alternative Route

Losehill Farm

Losehill Hall

START

The Castle

Castleton

Mam Tor
1696 ft

Windy Knoll

Peveril Castle

Cave Dale

Winnats Pass

half mile

past a lone tree leads out onto the northern side of the ridge where a steep, loose and eroded path ascends the edge. Once the distinctive tree-capped top is reached, the uninterrupted views across Kinder Scout make the hard work worth while, and it is a place to savour before the crowds are met again on Lose Hill.

This is but a short walk away along a level path – it steepens a little as it reaches the National Trust fence – and the path is again gritstone flags, a sure sign of heavy use! Atop the very summit is an orientation pillar outlining the view and various landmarks around, and a well engineered path leading down the southern slopes.

Upon leaving the NT area, take the right-hand path across the obvious stile, and downhill. Just before Losehill Farm is reached, a large finger-post points the way across a steep, grassy meadow – Castleton – or to the Lose Hill Larder at the farm. An ice cream or a pint in the village, what a choice! Whichever is chosen, the walk eventually must pass this way, so follow the frequent well sign-posted stiles across farmland. Just past Riding House Farm the track drops down wooden steps to a small bridge, crosses the stream and continues down to the surfaced road at Losehill Hall.

Turn right, and ignore the next left turn, to carry on through a gate and across a stile into a field. Another tiny stream is crossed, this time just above a small weir, and on to a gravel path where a cattle grid leads the way alongside the sports ground. This then comes out onto a 'road', which if followed leftwards soon leads back to Castleton where the river is traced back through the car park, and to 'The Castle' where the legs may be rested while the arm does a bit of work.

Walk 13: Southern Kinder

Distance: 8 miles (12.7km)

Height gained: 1558ft (475m)

Time: 4 to 5 hours.

Start: Edale car park OS Ref 124854

Terrain: Good paths, utilising less frequented ways up and down Kinder Scout. Some easy, avoidable scrambling may be encountered. Navigation may be difficult in mist, although plenty of escape routes exist.

Maps: OS Landranger Sheet 110 — Sheffield & Huddersfield area (1:50 000).

Public transport: BR at Edale and local buses.

The Nag's Head, Edale; tel: (01433) 670291

At the 'end of the road' in Edale and the beginning of The Pennine Way stands the dark gritstone Nag's Head. A free house, all are made very welcome in this ideally situated pub and food is available lunchtime and evening. There is a small outside seating area over-looking the gritstone built houses and the lower slopes of the hill – and accommodation is available, including self catering apartments. All within a stone's throw of Kinder Scout!

Southern Kinder

Kinder Scout's dark and crag lined southern face rises to 1981ft above the hamlet of Edale, and several popular routes pick their way to the vast peat-covered plateau. This route takes a little-used path to attain the top via an idyllic tumbling stream and an easily avoided simple scramble on the rough Kinder Scout grit. Once on top, a path round the rim takes the walker above some of the mighty gritstone crags on this side of the hill before descending the rugged spur of Ringing Roger or Echoing Rocks.

Kinder's lower slopes

The Walk

As parking in Edale is just about nonexistent it is necessary to start the walk from the car parks either just off the road or by the station. A mere ten minutes' walking to just before the Nag's Head, finds a footpath leading off to the left. This is the Pennine Way. A kissing gate leads to a well-engineered path in a cutting alongside a stream. Following a gate and a stile the way passes out into the meadow land on the lower slopes of Kinder and the route is followed pleasantly along flag-stones set into the grass.

This continues over stiles and pastures, until the path becomes more stony as an extensive area of land-slippage is approached, where a finger-post points the way to Crowden Brook. This will generally leave any crowds behind. Climb gently on a grassy path to a large iron kissing gate – this is the boundary of Open Country – then contour the hillside to a walled, wooded enclosure on the left. Here some height is lost by dropping to the stream bed then climbing back out, followed by an even bigger loss of height to the tumbling Crowden Brook.

This is one of the best paths on Kinder as it picks its way upwards, always accompanied by the music of the brook. It drops to water level, crosses and recrosses on the grippy gritstone boulders, all the while in an enchanting upland landscape. As height is gained the views become more wild and the way steeper and more rocky, until a path leads off leftwards towards the obvious crags on the skyline. Either follow this easily or, for a little more difficulty but far superior views, continue with the stream.

The path is still easy to follow, although now much less worn as it twists and turns through the boulders to the foot of the waterfall. This is not the impasse it seems. To the far left of the fall a very easy scramble can be found where a ladder-like series of foot- and hand-holds lead to just above the steep section of the fall (not recommended in winter, as the rocks can be iced with spray from the waterfall). It is easy once above the main fall to pick a path through the slabs and huge boulders that carry the stream from the top of Kinder Scout, the plateau of which is all too soon reached. Even without following the Clough direct, it is worth a trip to the

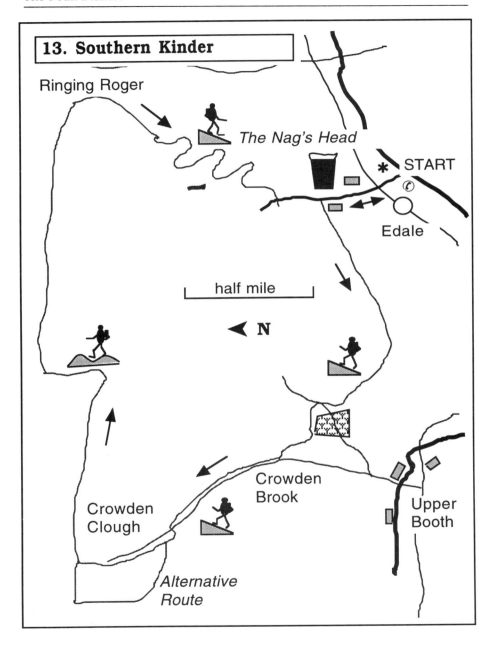

13. Southern Kinder

Ringing Roger

The Nag's Head

★ START

Edale

half mile

◄ N

Crowden Brook

Crowden Clough

Upper Booth

Alternative Route

foot of the falls, when a few minutes retracing you steps downhill will bring the easy path underfoot.

Once on top of Kinder the landscape changes. This is high moorland, and can be an unbelievably inhospitable place in winter. Almost Arctic in fact. However, a good path leads all the way round the rim, and this is followed rightwards along the very edge of the plateau. At a pair of distinctive rocks the required path branches off leftwards towards the top of the normal path from Edale in Grindsbrook. Here, there is a large scrappy cairn and crowds, which are soon left behind by continuing along the rim.

Above the eastern branch of Grindsbrook, the path goes first alongside one side of the ravine before dropping over rocks to the clough itself then climbing out and doubling back along the other side. All the while there are huge wind-sculpted towers guarding the edge. More of the same is the order of the day, as the path continues on top of the rim of crags towering above the heather slopes below. Soon an obvious path drops from the edge via Golden Clough – this is one alternative return route – although it is better to continue for a short distance to the spur of Ringing Roger.

Ringing Roger is said to mean Echoing Rocks, and these rocks are to be found at the end of the southward pointing ridge, reached by a sinuous path through heather and bracken. At the rocks a path may be found winding its way through the stepped buttresses until, after smaller bouldery outcrops, the path reaches the open hillside. A worn and loose track is followed steeply down to some zig-zags where it becomes a stepped and easy stairway to the valley below. At a stile a grassy path soon brings the main Grindsbrook track underfoot, where a drop onto a bridge and a corresponding climb brings the route back out among the houses of Edale where the Nag's Head is but a few strides away.

Walk 14: Kinder's Northern Edges

Distance: 9.5 or 12.1 miles (15.2/19.4km)

Height gained: 1086ft (331m)

Time: 4.5 to 7 hours.

Start: In lay-bys alongside Snake Road (A57), GR 113905. Or Birchin Clough car park, GR 110914.

Terrain: High moorland and rocky edges. One sometimes awkward stream crossing necessary for a longer route. The northern side of Kinder Scout is susceptible to bad weather and escape across Ashop Clough may be tricky.

Maps: OS Landranger Sheet 110 – Sheffield & Huddersfield area (1:50 000).

Public transport: BR between Bamford, Sheffield and Manchester, then buses across the Snake Pass.

The Snake Pass Inn, Snake Pass (A57); tel: (01433) 651480

All alone on the bleak Snake Road stands the welcoming stone building of the Snake Pass Inn. In summer it is bustling with people but, come winter, the main clientele is comprised of the hardy souls that have ventured onto this less-frequented side of Kinder. Dating from the 1820s, a Free House also serving good food, it has a walkers' bar as well as comfortable lounge bars. Children are made very welcome and dogs are allowed in the garden and into the lobby – where there are a few seats and some amazing photographs of the pass in winter. Accommodation ranges from comfortable rooms in the hotel to bunk-house type.

Northern Kinder Scout

It is hard to believe that the side of Kinder overlooking the Snake and Bleaklow, beyond, is the same hill as featured in walk 13. Totally lacking in the sunny disposition that the southern slopes

Winter-time crossing of the River Ashop

have, it is an often bleak rock and moorland landscape that welcomes the Pubhiker – just listen to how often the Snake Pass is blocked by snow. The walking here has a more serious feel to it, perhaps because of the sometimes deep ravine of Ashop Clough cutting off many otherwise easy escape routes; but this, coupled with the comparative scarcity of fellow hill-goers, endows the walking with a true mountain feel. Navigation may also be awkward beyond the end of the rocks, where the open moorland gives an inkling of the atmosphere on the interior of the huge plateau that makes up Kinder Scout.

The Walk

From the lay-by start off down the road for a few hundred metres to a stile set back behind the wall, marked as a footpath to Open Country. This goes down steps into the trees, crosses a small bridge, then just as the first rocks come into view, descends further to a good bridge crossing the stream. On the other side climb gently – now inside Open Country – and head towards the Fair Brook as it flows from the heights. This is decision time. The crossing, if easy, extends the walk significantly and makes for an excellent day's expedition, although if thwarted by high water, the path alongside the stream makes for an entertaining day in its own right.

Assuming the brook is crossed, continue up the diagonally ascending path across the broad shoulder to the course of Gate Side Clough. This is then followed upwards passing a stream on the right, the incut of which makes a pleasant spot for a short break, to a broken wall, then on to the rim path at Seal Stones. A right turn is made and the rim is followed above Seal Edge to the huge defile of the Fair Brook, with Fairbrook Naze jutting out into the rough moorland.

If the path up Fair Brook is followed, simply climb very gently alongside the stream up the obvious path. This, at times, is quite high above the stream, and small streams enter from both right and left, until an old tree, growing almost horizontally out of the bank, is reached. Here the path becomes narrow and slightly awkward in places, and the views to the crag-girt rim of the hill are enough to reduce concentration. Beyond, the moorland opens out and the path continues to follow the water to a rougher, more bouldery area. From here all that remains is to follow the jumbled mass of boulders to the very rim, where the Fair Brook issues from the peat morass.

Once on Fairbrook Naze, navigation could not be easier. There is a huge area of tussocky moorland to the left, and black rounded gritstone crags and tors to the right. The eroded path picks its way between these natural barriers and gives superlative walking for about 2.5 miles to the very end of the rocks at the aptly named Boxing Glove Rocks, although be sure en-route to look out for the amazing protruding block of Punch's Nose on Ashop Edge, the line of an excellent rock climb.

When the rocks have finished, the open moorland gives a taster of what the open top of the hill is like, as poor paths pick their way through the heather. All of a sudden, the western edge is reached, and below are the large Kinder Reservoir and the path coming up from Glossop. Turn right here – this is part of the Pennine Way –

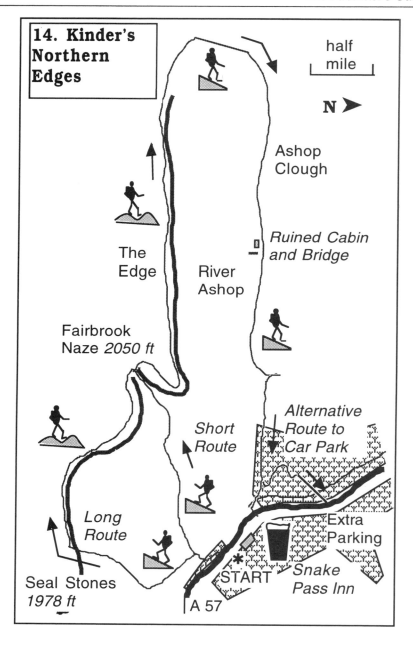

14. Kinder's Northern Edges

half mile

N ▶

Ashop Clough

Ruined Cabin and Bridge

The Edge

River Ashop

Fairbrook Naze *2050 ft*

Alternative Route to Car Park

Short Route

Long Route

Extra Parking

Snake Pass Inn

Seal Stones *1978 ft*

START

A 57

cross a stile, and drop steeply on the open hillside to another stile. Just beyond this is a sign, and this must be the only signpost for a pub on any hill. Do not get too excited though, there is still a long way to go! When this book was being written, this section of path was being repaired with gritstone slabs, so much of the boggy, bare peat should be long past by the time you use it.

Follow the sign rightwards and start the long descent alongside the infant River Ashop. Paved at first it winds gently down, with the river but a trickle on the right-hand side. Currently the repaired path soon disappears however, and as the river gains in magnitude and small feeders cross the path the way may be more than a little boggy. This goes on for what seems like ever before a glimpse of the forests surrounding the pub come into view, then down at river level a small ruined cabin and a plank bridge are passed just opposite Upper Gate Clough (this provides a convenient crossing point if shortening the latter part of the rim walk). Continue along the river, dropping steeply into the small ravine of Nether Gate Clough, then on to the stile on the edge of the woodland.

A narrow path goes through the conifers, and continues down towards the Snake Pass Inn, or, if parked in the public car park follow the signposted forest walk. The way is shown, first by white waymarking, then blue and white and finally blue before it emerges onto the road at a steep little climb. Whichever way is taken, the pub and a good pint are just a few minutes away.

The Shropshire Hills

Passed by many of the hill-going population, as they speed westwards to the more famous peaks of Wales, the hills of Shropshire are hidden gems. Although of modest height, some have a character more akin to the mountains of Snowdonia than to the moorland of the North Midlands. They are the much loved 'Blue Remembered Hills' of A. E. Houseman, author of 'A Shropshire Lad', and are some of my favourite hill areas.

Covering approximately 300 square miles, they offer the discerning walker a haven of peace when more popular areas are sorely crowded. They take the form of three long parallel ridges with scattered hill groups surrounding them. The eastern most ridge, Wenlock Edge, is a limestone plateau overlooking a narrow plain. In the centre is an area of wild moorland that would do justice to the Pennines – The Long Mynd – six miles by four, it rears to about 1700 feet (518m) and is cut by many deep and narrow valleys, and in winter can be a bleak and inhospitable place. It offers superlative walking (see route 15), centred mainly on Church Stretton, which is also an ideal centre to avail oneself of the delightful Caer Caradoc hills.

Finally, and the location of walk 16, lies the long rocky ridge of The Stiperstones, Shropshire's second highest point at 1762 feet (537m). Steeped in legend, the summit rocks are said to be frequented by the Devil and haunted by the ghost of the Saxon, Edric Sylvaticus – Wild Edric – who is said to be seen on the eve of the country going to war. Whatever, the scattered quartzite crags along the ridge give a fine walk, with the added interest of the lead mine remains at Snailbeach. The other Shropshire hills also afford fine walking, with Brown Clee Hill being the highest at 1790ft (546m), while in the north of the group stands the remote Wrekin, with an Iron Age hill fort on its summit.

Owing to the compact nature of the hills and the scarcity of human habitation, Shropshire perhaps offers less to the Pubhiker than some other areas, although there are sufficient opportunities to make a visit worthwhile. Real ale is to be found in most outlets, and there are eight real ale breweries in the county, several of which are in, or close to the hills. One of these, away from the walking area (but near the Blist's Hill Museum) is the All Nations, a brew pub dating back about two centuries, which makes All Nations Pale Ale – the only draught product on sale.

Although compact in area, two OS maps are recommended: Landranger 1: 50 000 – Sheets 126 and 137 (walk 15 may be done with just Sheet 126).

Walk 15: The Long Mynd

Distance: 11 miles (17.6km)

Height gained: 1200ft (366m)

Time: 3 to 5 hours.

Start: Limited discreet parking in Little Stretton village OS Ref 443918 (alternative start at 'High Park' GR 421954)

Terrain: Some narrow and surprisingly rocky paths alongside streams, moorland tracks and some quiet roads.

Maps: OS Landranger Sheet 137 – Ludlow, Wenlock Edge and surrounding area (1:50 000).

Public transport: BR at Shrewsbury and Church Stretton. Buses run to Little Stretton village.

The Ragleth Inn, Little Stretton; tel: (01694) 722711

Nestling among the green Southern Shropshire hills, the village of Little Stretton is now by-passed by the main A49 road, which means that the 400 year old Ragleth Inn is in a peaceful backwater. The brick and tile building blends in with the surrounding houses and the bracken-covered slopes of the Long Mynd and the setting must be little changed from when it was built. Walkers, their children and their dogs are all welcomed in the Public Bar with its unusual red brick floor and warm coal stove in the winter months. Food is available lunchtime and evenings along with ales from Marstons, as well as a guest beer. The pub also offers accommodation and has a large garden to the side with magnificent views of the surrounding hills.

The Long Mynd

Between Wenlock Edge and the ridge of the Stiperstones lies the great mass of high moorland of the Long Mynd. Reaching 1692ft (516m) at Pole Bank, it is unusual in so much as two roads cross its huge expanse of moorland – more reminiscent of the Pennines. The eastern aspect of the hill displays several deep valleys, each with their own character. The Carding Mill Valley is tourist territory but the area around here is less frequented, and the ascent by Ashes Hollow can even provide a little simple scrambling. There is a comparatively long section of road walking on this route, although the roads are narrow and quiet – the last time I walked the route, shortly before publication, we were passed by only three cars! The road walking can be minimised by using other routes back to the valley.

The Walk

Take the lane alongside the Ragleth Inn and continue to its end, where a small stream is to be found – this stream is a constant companion in the first stage of the walk as it is followed to its source high on the moorlands above. Turn right and cross a ford by a small footbridge, then take the stile immediately right into the pasture. This is, in season, a camping field and few more idyllic places to pitch a tent in the English Midlands can be imagined. Beyond another stile, the footpath leads across pastures on a grassy surface to the boundary of the National Trust property. From here, the valley winds away in front with a footbridge next to the derelict house, Ashes.

Drop to the level of the stream and pass under the gnarled old oak tree on its bank. Further on, the valley begins to narrow and more bare rock is evident among the bracken until the path is forced across the stream. Where the stream falls over a few rock steps the way is partially barred by a rocky outcrop and an easy scramble is necessary to continue. Cross again and scramble over a small buttress about eight feet (2.5m) above the water, and on to a small ridge of rock, again providing a little entertainment.

Just beyond this, a magnificent holly almost blocks the stream and the way continues up the rocks to a, now excellent, path climbing

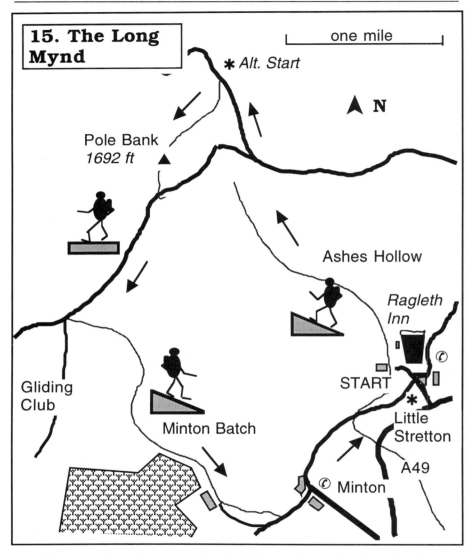

15. The Long Mynd

one mile

✱ *Alt. Start*

▲ N

Pole Bank
1692 ft ▲

Ashes Hollow

Ragleth Inn

Gliding
Club

START

✱

Little
Stretton

Minton Batch

A49

ⓒ Minton

gently away from the water level. Where the path splits, the lower one gives an enjoyable little scramble above a small fall, while the upper follows an easy 'no hands' path. The path soon levels as the dale opens out and swings to the right. The way is all uphill, on a sometimes intermittent path, to emerge abruptly at the road.

Ashes Hollow

Turn right for a few minutes, then left following the sign to the Youth Hostel. This is now bare moorland, with to the left, the trig point on the very top of the Long Mynd. Suddenly, a magnificent panorama of the long Stiperstones ridge bursts into view with the hills of Wales spread out beyond, and the High Park car park (Optional Start) is reached. Take the broad track on the left across the windswept plateau which quickly leads to the trig point and view-indicator. From the top the view is magnificent. The Arans in Wales, Brown Clee Hill – the highest point in Shropshire, the Malverns and on a clear day the hills of the Peak District are all spread out around the horizon.

Leave the top by the good track leading towards the stand of trees obvious to the south. This comes out again on the road, and the next mile and a bit follows this towards The Midlands Gliding Club, although there are several routes back to either Little Stretton or Minton that shorten the walk by varying amounts. Just before the access road to the gliding club, bear left across boggy ground and head for the narrow valley of Minton Batch. Trackless at first, a narrow path is soon picked up leading into the steep-sided dell. Wind down alongside the embryo stream to a lone tree with an enigmatic notice nailed to it and, just beyond, a small rock buttress.

Easier and less rugged than the path taken to the top of the hill, it is also a little boggier and with more trees. A forest is immediately in front, and easy walking leads across bouldery scree, then grass to another easy to follow track alongside the river. From here the walking is pleasant and easy, first alongside the forest, then around Shooters Knoll, past the farm and on to a cattle grid. Here, either take the bridleway signposted through the gate a few feet up the hillside or continue along the farm track.

Both ways lead to a narrow lane where a left turn is taken into the hamlet of Minton. Take the road past the telephone box and continue pleasantly downhill towards the prominent Ragleth Hill signposted to Little Stretton. The village comes into view just after a ford and footbridge – as does the rugged Caer Caradoc Hill – and just a few minutes walking, then a right turn brings the garden of the Ragleth Inn into view. A beer in the garden soon has any tiredness forgotten, and a glance at the map has more plans made. Perhaps Caer Caradoc next?

Walk 16: Stiperstones Ridge and the Devil's Chair

Distance: 8.5 miles (13.5km)

Height gained: 1256ft (383m)

Time: 3 to 4 hours.

Start: Discreet parking in the village, beware very narrow roads, OS Ref 373021 (alternative start at Stiperstones car park GR 370977)

Terrain: Tracks and paths, generally good, the ridge is rocky and rough in places.

Maps: OS Landranger Sheet 126 – Shrewsbury and surrounding area and Sheet 137 – Ludlow, Wenlock Edge and surrounding area (1:50 000).

Public transport: BR at Shrewsbury. Buses run to Stiperstones village.

The Stiperstones Inn, Stiperstones; tel: (01743) 791327

The setting of The Stiperstones Inn is a revelation to anyone not familiar with Shropshire's hills. It nestles beneath a deep dingle running down from the ridge and, as such, is used to the diversity of outdoor people passing through. The public bar, with a fire in winter, must be one of the most welcoming places for a walker. Good food is available all day, as is beer from the local Wood's brewery, and there is even a shop and post office attached! Children and dogs are also welcomed. Very well priced accommodation is also available, both at the Inn and self-catering.

The Stiperstones

The Stiperstones, a narrow ridge of gleaming quartzite, owe more to the rugged hills of Wales, than the more rounded type usually found in Central England. Surrounded by legend, Shropshire's second highest point gives an excellent day's hillwalking in an area not usually explored by most people. The route described is the best one to the ridge, as it takes in all the different aspects of the hill – although a more direct (and higher) start may be made at the car park (see alternative start). The walking is generally on good paths, although the actual ridge itself is quite rugged. It is on the ridge that the quartzite outcrops, in a line of scale-like crags. One of these, Manstone Rock contains the trig point of the second highest point in Shropshire (1758ft, 536m), although it is The Devil's Chair that is perhaps better known. It is said that on days of mist the Devil himself sits atop the hill, while the headless ghost of Edric the Red haunts the crags if the country is about to go to war. Perhaps it is best to not seek out either!

On the Stiperstones ridge

The Walk

From the pub turn right down the road, and follow this quiet lane pleasantly through the hamlet of Snailbeach as far as the turning for Lord's Hill. Here a new footpath on the left-hand side cuts off a short section of road, to re-emerge by the recently restored lead mine buildings (well worth investigation). Walk past these, and climb steeply through woodland, on a rapidly deteriorating surface to emerge from the gloom just as the track levels out.

In front is another mine chimney, and just by a gate a secretive chapel with its attendant graveyard, pass these and continue to a point where several bridleways lead off. Take the right hand of these, which has a good surface, and follow it uphill. The view makes a good excuse for a rest, The Wrekin in the distance and nearer to hand, the rounded top of Pontesbury Hill. The walking now has the feel of a true upland path, the panorama to the right improving with every step.

The route is easy to follow, as only one track keeps to the broad back of the ridge, all deviations being ignored. Passing through a narrow band of trees the green pastureland begins to give way to heathery moorland, and the Stiperstones Nature Reserve (dogs must be on leads). To the right, the fingers of ridge reach out to the valley while beyond, patchwork fields give way to hills; in the distance, the mountains of Wales can be seen, with overhead, the croak of ravens or the characteristic mewling of buzzards.

The path becomes stonier as the rugged quartzite spine of the hill begins to rise in front. On a misty day, it is easy to believe in the Devil, but when the sun shines all such thoughts are banished by the twinkling of the quartz bringing the very path alive. The Devil's Chair is the first major outcrop to be passed, with shortly afterwards the trig point crowned Manstone Rock – the second highest point in Shropshire – where an easy scramble brings the very top to hand, the panorama making it all worth while.

The tors, said to have been scattered by Lucifer himself, begin to diminish as the path begins to descend. The going remains rough, until suddenly the rocks give way to a smooth grassy carpet dipping through the heathery moorland. The best views are now to the left,

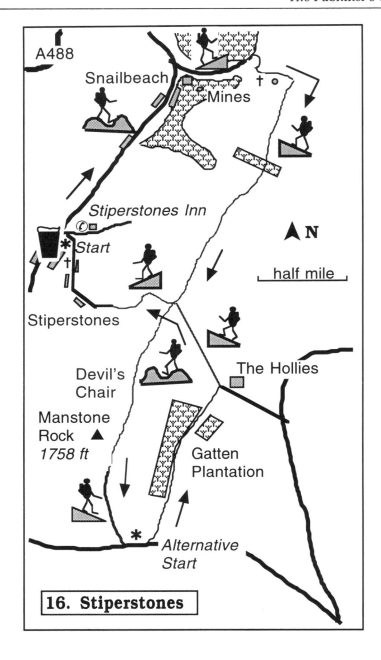

A488

Snailbeach Mines

Stiperstones Inn

Start

Stiperstones

N

half mile

Devil's
Chair

The Hollies

Manstone
Rock ▲
1758 ft

Gatten
Plantation

*Alternative
Start*

16. Stiperstones

across the East Onney valley to the deeply indented flanks of the Long Mynd, and they help to speed the way to the car park (Alternative Start).

At the car park turn sharp left and pass through a gate onto a track leading towards the dark Gatten Plantation. Once in the trees, the path although good is, in a couple of places, kept wet by the resurgence of springs, one always lightly flooding the area by a final gate. After the gate the way is marked with hand-painted signs as it crosses the sheep-cropped meadows of The Hollies, and is directed half-left, uphill to re-enter the Reserve at a gate where the path signed as Wild Edric's Way is followed.

Follow the path past an untidy cairn, cross the ridge and descend into Perkin's Beach. This is open and grassy at first, but soon descends into a worn and narrow path as the steep ridges enclosing the dingle press in. Soon however, the track becomes better and occasional cottages begin to appear, while further down, the way becomes surfaced. It is now but a short distance to the Stiperstones Inn and that welcoming drink.

Wales

The hills of Wales are among the most varied in Britain, spreading as they do almost the whole length of the country. Unfortunately, the real ale picture is not quite so rosy. Until recently the live product was rarely to be found at all, although now most of the tourist areas are well served, and supply is spreading. The walks in this section are to be found in the north of the country, where the magnet of Snowdonia draws walkers and climbers from far and wide. This is not to say that worthwhile walking does not exist outside the National Park; there is one walk in the book on the 'lesser' hills, which is no less enjoyable.

The first hills of note encountered by any visitor to Wales entering from Shropshire or Cheshire are the Clwydians – see route 17. These still wild and surprisingly unfrequented hills stretch roughly from the A5 up to the north coast and their heathery heights and steep limestone escarpments contain many hidden gems. They are also traversed by the Offa's Dyke Path as it follows the English/Welsh border on its way to the sea.

The honey-pot as far as Welsh hill walking is concerned has to be Snowdonia. Britain's second largest National Park also contains England and Wales' highest mountain – Snowdon – as well as the bulk of 3000 feet (915m) plus summits outside Scotland. This is mountain country – bare rocks, rushing cascades and sometimes fearsome drops, all thrown up by volcanic upheaval about 400 million years ago, then shaped by two major ice-ages and thousands of years of erosion into the landscape so admired today.

Many of the valleys are without significant habitation, so dedicated pub-walkers must choose their centres carefully. It was not always so – hotels existed in such remote places as the Gorphywysfa Hotel at Pen-y-Pass, and in the Ogwen Valley. These, however, are long closed, and some now function as Youth Hostels; several, in a novel twist of fate, are again licensed to sell wine and beer with meals. No real ale though!

The main mountain ranges relevant to this section are the great whale-backs of the Carneddau, the northernmost hills. Barren, grassy ridges characterise these mountains, and although most access points are rather remote from pubs, it is possible to venture onto their lofty slopes from the village of Capel Curig, and the following walk gives a good taster of what these less trampled peaks offer.

The next group southwards is the Glydderau and here lies what is Snowdonia's most impressive peak, Tryfan at 3010 feet (917m) – a remote and noble mountain rearing high above the A5. The bulk of the range comprises the more rounded Glyders, Fawr and Fach, both well over 3000 feet, and with tops bristling with bare rock. This group of peaks may be reached either from the shores of Llyn Ogwen or as outlined in this book from Nant Peris, and good navigation is a desirable attribute in the not infrequent poor visibility; quite a few people manage to descend into the wrong valley!

Further south still is the jewel in North Wales' crown, Snowdon itself. Yr Wyddfa, as it is known in Welsh, is really a massif of nine high peaks with Snowdon itself forming the centrepiece. Somewhat defaced by the cafe and with the terminus for the rack and pinion steam railway, it remains a valid goal. Once off the summit, especially on some of the less popular routes, the walker may be alone with only the cry of the ravens as company. An ascent of Snowdon must be in every visitor to the area's heart; the walk featured herein (No. 22) shows completely different aspects of the hill, and can happily be finished with a beer.

Most of the beers available in the pubs and hotels of North Wales are from English breweries. The county of Clwyd, however, has a couple of its own, and other areas of Wales have local brewers, so although there is unlikely to be any new beer experiences, the quality of the walking more than compensates.

The following maps will be found useful: OS Landranger (1:50 000) sheets 116 Denbigh & Colwyn Bay area and 115 Caernarvon & Bangor.

Walk 17: Moel Famau

Distance: 12 miles (19.2km)

Height gained: 2320ft (710m)

Time: 5 to 6 hours.

Start: Moel Famau Car Park. GR 161605.

Terrain: Good paths, generally well signposted, although there is a deceptive amount of 'up and down'.

Maps: OS Landranger Sheet 116 – Denbigh and Colwyn Bay area (1:50 000).

Public transport: None.

White Horse, Cilcain; tel: (01352) 740142

It is a real pleasure to find a thriving pub in a tiny village such as Cilcain and the low, white painted White Horse is perfectly situated to split the walk and enjoy a beer. There is a lounge where meals are served and a small walkers' bar (with an interesting beer engine) as well as a compact outside seating area, where children and dogs are allowed – on a sunny day, this is a veritable sun-trap. It is a free-house, serving a variety of ales and good food.

Offa's Dyke

Offa's Dyke path traverses much of the Clwydian Range. The defensive dyke was built to keep the Welsh from England and was the work of the Mercian Saxon King Offa in the 8th century. Much of the hilly part of this walk uses paths on the line of the earthwork; the first hill is Foel Fenlli, crowned by its ancient hill-fort – one of many in the area. The final 'sting in the tail' is Moel Famau (Mother Mountain) at 1818ft (554m), which is crowned by the stump of the Jubilee Tower, which was built in 1810 to celebrate the Golden Jubilee of George III.

The White Horse, Cilcain

The Walk

Leave the car park in a southerly direction and, almost immediately, start the ascent of the steep slopes of Foel Fenlli. This is a stony path that zig-zags to a stile from where the path is stepped. The labour is eased by the fine views that open out; to the right are the distant hills of Snowdonia, while behind are the gaunt remains of the Jubilee Tower on Moel Famau. Soon, a slight ridge is reached with a good path leading to the hill-fort atop Foel Fenlli (1676ft, 511m) where a path winding through bilberries leads to the cairn.

Many paths lead to the foot of the hill and a stile alongside a wood, where a rising path and more stiles lead around the trees and into a pasture. Follow the field edge to another stile by a small wood and continue straight on to a bridleway. Turn left here, leaving the Offa's Dyke path, then right onto another bridleway between a wall and fence, again alongside a wood. The track soon becomes roughly surfaced with good views across to the small limestone outcrops over the valley, and is followed past several cattle-grids to the A494.

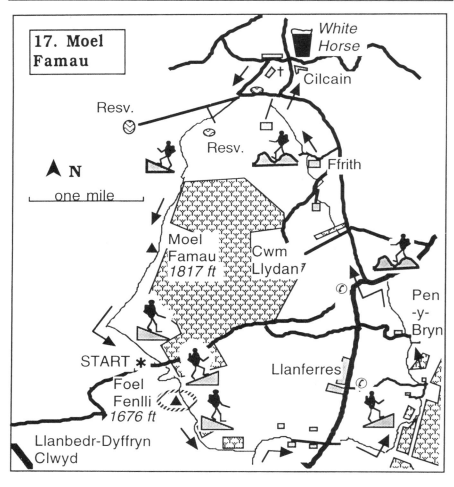

17. Moel Famau

White Horse

Cilcain

Resv.

Resv.

Ffrith

N

one mile

Moel Famau *1817 ft*

Cwm Llydan

Pen -y- Bryn

START *

Foel Fenlli *1676 ft*

Llanferres

Llanbedr-Dyffryn Clwyd

Cross the road and take the signposted footpath opposite which leads gently down to the river. Cross the bridge and continue along the, now grassy, path as it curves round to the right, then climbs to the obvious wood in front. Walk alongside the wood on a barely trodden path to a short rise and a gate and stile marked with a yellow arrow. More trackless walking leads around a cottage to another gate and a gravel path past the building, then onto the 'white road'. Turn left, and cross the stile on the bend and take the rustic footpath past the house to another stile giving out onto a meadow. This gives pleasant walking across fields – the hunting grounds of the local buzzard population whose plaintive cries often accompany you – and a series of stiles soon drops the path down to meet the Afon Alun again, where it leads out to the road at a bridge and ford.

Cross the bridge and take the footpath on the other side of the river where the way is indicated by a sign reading "This is my garden so lovingly planted. A gift to me which God has granted. As you walk may it bring you laughter and smiles. Please keep your dog on a lead between stiles". It is a strange feeling to walk across the end of a person's garden! Just over the stile, the path is furnished with a fallen tree trunk, a pleasant place to sit alongside the stream and garden.

Pass through a kissing-gate and continue along the well-defined path above the river to another gate and an arch. Climb briefly and cross the track then continue the other side to a brook crossed by a stone slab. The next section traverses paddocks; it is well way-marked and well provided with gates, and soon leads again to the A494. Turn left and then almost immediately right at the next lane – signposted to Cilcain – where just ten minutes of walking has the next footpath showing on the left.

This starts off well-surfaced, although the way we want soon crosses the river on the right. It immediately passes through a boggy area to a stile, then across stepping stones to emerge from the trees with a superb view up to the forested cwm of Moel Famau. A series of stiles leads across meadows to the farm, then the road. Here, turn right and follow the narrow lane to a bridleway on the left. This is taken to Ffrith where a footpath drops very steeply to the fields below – this is very easy to miss – and a series of stiles leading towards the squat church of Cilcain. Once on the road, go first downhill, then steeply up, to the pub. Most welcome!

From the White Horse, walk past the church and take the first road on the left. At a sharp bend, by the 'Welsh Water' buildings, cross a stile onto the grass footpath, which is followed to the bridleway, and continue in the same direction. Stony at first, then grassy as it climbs through woods and past a small reservoir to a wooden sign where it suddenly becomes a footpath. Here, after a short level section, the path starts to zig-zag up the broad flanks of the hill aiming for the obvious skyline. This unfortunately is merely a false summit, although the stump of the Jubilee Tower is now visible in front and just 300 feet (91m) higher. Soon reached!

Either rest a while on top and admire the extensive views, or take the obvious wide path around the western flank of the hill. This gives very easy walking on a sound base and overlooks the small town of Ruthin, and the hill-fort of Moel-y-Gaer and with the more impressive ramparts of Foel Fenlli in front. As it nears the road, it swings to the left and descends to the car park where there is often a food kiosk.

Walk 18: Moel Hebog

Distance: 5.75 miles (9.2km)

Height gained: 2430ft (741m)

Time: 4.5 to 6 hours.

Start: Beddgelert Car Park. GR 590481.

Terrain: Reasonable paths, some cairned. The upper part of the mountain is very rocky. Steep grassy descent to forest, then interesting forest paths

Maps: OS Landranger Sheet 115 – Caernarvon & Bangor (1:50 000).

Public transport: Local, and Snowdon Sherpa buses in season.

The Royal Goat, Beddgelert; tel: (01766) 890224

The best starting place is the public car park (pay and display), just round the corner from The Royal Goat. This is a large building on a bend of the A498 at the very edge of the small village of Beddgelert. A warm welcome awaits walkers in its imposing bar overlooking the village. Children are welcome, although dogs are allowed no further than the pleasant patio area outside the hotel. As would be expected of a hotel, both accommodation and food are available.

Moel Hebog

Moel Hebog totally dominates the village of Beddgelert, and rears up immediately behind the Royal Goat Hotel – its 2566ft (782m) summit is just one and three quarter miles away. This means a steep climb! It is an underrated hill although attaining the summit is never tedious, with views that are as good as any in Snowdonia, taking in Snowdon and her satellites as well as the Moelwyns and even the Glyderau. Beyond this there are magnificent views out to sea, along the Llyn Peninsular and even as far as Cader Idris.

The Walk

Leave the car park, where an information board may be found, and turn right, take the small road past the side of the hotel, and ascend gently through a cluster of white painted houses. Here is found a footpath sign showing the way up some steps and across the old disused narrow gauge railway to a 'walking man' sign. Follow these signs across pastures, through an old iron gate and on to a gate and a walled track. Turn right, signposted to Cwm Cloch and follow it as it winds through derelict farm buildings, and eventually, just after a stream, to a ladder stile alongside an old barn.

The meadow the other side can be boggy, as the drains testify. It

Approaching Moel Hebog

is short, however, and another ladder stile by a sheep-fold has firmer ground underfoot. Here the ascent proper begins and a grassy saddle is soon reached at the first of the cairns. From here the views are quite incredible. Snowdon, along the Gwynant Valley, Cnicht and the Moelwyns, with nestling in the valley Beddgelert clustered around its major road junction, well worth taking a breather!

Grassy paths lead onwards and upwards with occa-

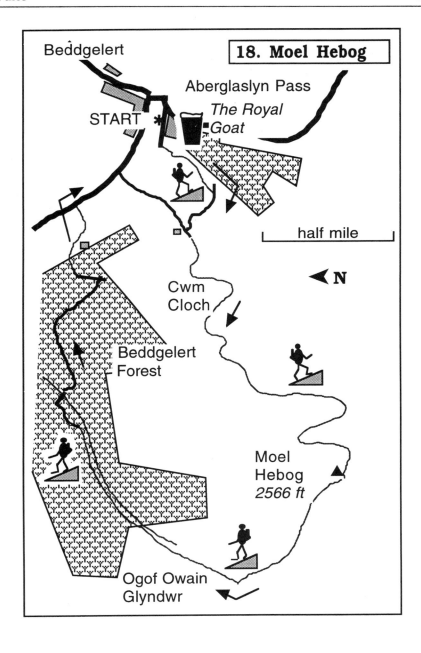

sional signs to help find the way, while the main bulk of the mountain stands resolutely in front. After a final wall and stile the path begins to take on a more mountainous character. Rocks and boulders to the sides, and soon underfoot, mark an end to the lower reaches of the hill and draw the walker on to the steeper and more interesting paths ahead. Widely spaced cairns mark the path, though some are difficult to distinguish from the bare rock so prevalent hereabouts, and it is just this rock that imbues the route with a 'scrambly' character, with hands occasionally coming into play.

Continue up the broad shoulder to a scree chute beneath an easy angled gully with a cairn at its base. This gives a few feet of very mild scrambling to reach rough zig-zags easing the angle of the climb to a small rise, beyond which the sea suddenly bursts into view with Cardigan Bay stretching away into the distance. Just after a particularly steep twisting section, where the path turns abruptly to the left, the way leads through some remarkable rock formations. Soon loose scree carries the path around the bubbly rock, and then to small buttresses with the grey crags rearing up to the left.

As a final rocky tower is crested the summit ridge of Moel Hebog is reached, and the views open out over the Llyn Peninsular with the Rivals a prominent landmark. From here, a great swelling slope leads alongside the void on the left to the trig point and summit wall. Last time I was here, my wife and I were confronted with a pack of baying hounds racing towards us. Fortunately they were following a scent, and were totally oblivious to our presence, as they raced away in the direction of our recent ascent.

From the summit, descend alongside the wall (right-hand side) over steep grass with an intermittent path – these slopes could be very dangerous when frozen or covered in snow, so care, or even a descent by the ascent route may be needed. A very quick – hopefully controlled – descent leads over a couple of small rocky areas and to a broken-down dry-stone wall with a ladder stile on the right. The rocks above, on Moel yr Ogof, contain the cave where Owen Glyndwr is said to have hidden from the English. Unless a detour is to be made to the cave, then follow the wall downhill to a prominent prow overlooking the forest. Immediately below is a ladder stile.

Crossing this plunges the route into the gloom of the forested Cwm Meillionen and the path descends steeply over slippery rocks to a forest road. Cross this and dive again into the forest where the path drops to join a stream, and a route has to be picked through the various boggy areas – sometimes the actual stream bed is the driest option! Cross another track and negotiate more bogs to yet another forest road.

The next section is a delight. As the ground drops away, so the stream falls in a series of cascades and the path winds its way excitingly alongside, fording another stream entering from the left before coming out onto another track. Here, it is possible to continue alongside the stream, but preferable to follow the battered yellow arrow and turn left. This gives superb views of Snowdon, the Moelwyns and a great retrospective of Moel Hebog, now high above, although it is important to remember that this is a working forest and the trees are often felled and replanted, so changing certain aspects.

At the next junction turn right, and at a tee-junction right again to cross the stream again. The way bears left alongside the edge of the trees with more pastoral land in view in the valley. At a fork by a ruined sheep-fold take the left-hand option and swing round to the footpath crossing – this point may also be reached by an overgrown path branching off at the actual sheep-fold. The next part of the footpath cannot really be avoided however, and it is time to plunge rightwards onto the very scrappy track. Boggy and covered in debris from tree-felling it leads gently down to the remains of a kissing-gate by a large Rhododendron bush and across a track.

Another gate (please close) that has seen better days, leads into a pasture by some buildings. Walk half right towards the far right-hand corner of the field where a ladder-stile crosses a wall. Ignore the stile, and find the gated foot-bridge across the Afon Colwyn (hidden from immediate view) and then walk up the field on the far side to the gate leading to the A4085. Beddgelert is then just a short stroll away – a quick route to the car park and the Royal Goat recrosses the river and skirts the school buildings to eventually emerge onto the A498.

Walk 19: Moel Siabod

Distance: 8.8 miles (14km)

Height gained: 2300ft (701m)

Time: 4 to 6 hours.

Start: Capel Curig Car Park. GR 721582.

Terrain: Good paths, steep ridge may provide easy scramble (path also exists). Very rough summit, navigation may be awkward in bad weather, although an easy and safe option may be taken direct to Plas-y-Brenin.

Maps: OS Landranger Sheet 115 – Caernarvon & Bangor (1:50 000).

Public transport: Buses from Llandudno to Llanberis and Llanwrst to Bangor.

Cobden's Hotel, Capel Curig; tel: (01690) 720243

Cobden's Hotel has a long tradition as a climbers' and walkers' meeting place, and their Clogwyn Bar continues this custom – although all are welcome in the Hotel's main bar. The Clogwyn Bar is built into the hillside and one wall is formed by the natural granite rock face, and is worth a visit for this alone. Situated alongside the Afon Llugwy the hotel makes a fine base for any number of excursions. It is a free-house with accommodation and a wide selection of good food and beer – on my last visit there was a new ale from the new Cambrian Brewery. Children and dogs are also made most welcome.

Moel Siabod

Moel Siabod (2861ft, 872m) is one of the best view-points in Snowdonia – a lowish outlying peak, although still with a definite mountain atmosphere. It is remote enough from the main mountain groups to give the walker a fine panorama of all three major areas, and, with the route outlined, forms a good introduction to the slightly tougher aspects of hillwalking, with the advantage that all difficulties may be avoided if the walker so wishes.

Cobden's from Moel Siabod

The Walk

From Cobden's cross the road and take the bridge above the Llugwy, where a gate at the end leads out onto the hillside. Turn left and follow paths over the rocky bluff in front to a ladder stile at a field edge. This is taken, and the river is followed to a stream crossing and a short rise to the old A5 by Bont Cyfyng. The river makes a fine sight, especially in times of spate, and is worth a look before turning briefly right up the road, where a cattle-grid shows the way up a steep track to the right.

Follow the track, dogs must be on leads, steadily upwards through trees. Where it curves to the right take the new path straight ahead. If you thought the last bit was steep, "You ain't seen nothing yet". As it curves to the right, magnificent views over the Carneddau unfold, and it joins the old path again at a cottage. Turn left and follow the good track over a ladder stile. As height is gained Moel Siabod dominates the view ahead, its massive East Face and the ridge of Daiar Ddu foremost.

After another, single, ladder stile a pair is reached. Take the left-hand one and continue on the good path cresting a slight rise. Below are the dark waters of a small lake constantly on the left as the path traverses about eight feet (2.5m) above the water line only to rise rockily towards the old quarries. First a ruined hut, then another short rise and the quarry proper is reached. A small cluster of ruins and an impressive water-filled hole fire the imagination, a good place to take a breather and, on a stormy day, the last chance to get out of the wind!

Leave the quarry by a steep path leading to the left-hand corner of the pit, where a small water-fall tumbles in, and follow the footpath sign on the fence. Now a short climb gently uphill on wet ground soon leads to the obvious col where a superb view of the Moelwyns opens out. In the immediate foreground, however, is Siabod's East Ridge, climbing in jagged isolation straight to the summit of the mountain. Before the delights of this however, the floor of the cwm has to be crossed. This is wet and there seems no reliable way across, but is mercifully short and the foot of the rocks is soon reached.

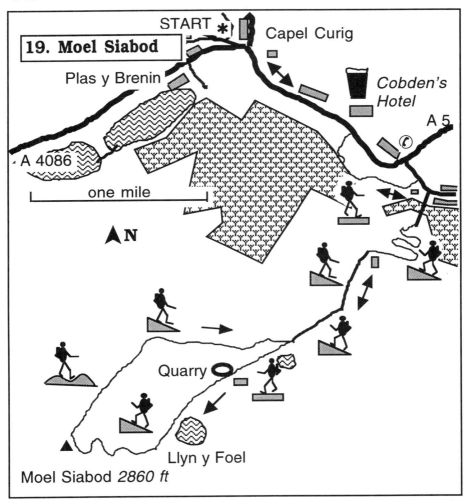

START

19. Moel Siabod

Plas y Brenin

Capel Curig

Cobden's Hotel

A 5

A 4086

one mile

▲N

Quarry

Llyn y Foel

Moel Siabod *2860 ft*

Walk around the bottom of the ridge and follow a narrow and winding path through the rocks and onto the ridge itself. This may be made as hard as you wish. There is always a path snaking through the buttresses, or they may all be taken direct, and the way is obvious, marked by crampon scratches and worn to an ochre sheen by the passage of many feet. It is worth pausing en-route and looking down into the Lledr Valley where the gaunt keep of Dolwyddelan Castle may be seen and the pass winds away to Blaenau Ffestiniog.

About half way up the ridge a step down onto a grassy ledge may prove intimidating as the drop snaps at your heels. There is nothing difficult, although the thought of a slide into the cwm does not bear thinking about. After a short flat section the rocks climb again, although much more broken than before, and many paths now lead through the outcrops. If the far right-hand side is followed, an excellent final and exposed scramble can be found on the very edge. Either taking this or the paths to the left soon brings the summit to hand.

The views from the top are some of the best in Snowdonia, with all the main mountain groups shown to their best, especially the majestic curving form of Snowdon and her satellites. Just to the north of the cairn is a large round wind-shelter ideal for a spot of lunch, and justifiably popular.

The best descent is to follow the blunt north-east ridge of the mountain. This gives easy scrambling up, down and around grey buttresses, all the time with fine views – a narrow path along the base of the rocks may also be taken. In mist, this is a safe and easy route off, as the actual spine of the ridge is difficult to lose. All too soon, however, the rocks run out into the grassy flanks of the hillside where a very loose gully leads down for 100 feet (30m) or so to the smooth slopes below.

At a line of shattered rocks, either follow their crest along a very feint path or drop into the damp gully to their right. This is loose and unpleasant but short, and leads to flatter walking across a soggy meadow to the second of the twin stiles mentioned earlier. All that remains is to follow the track back down towards Capel Curig perhaps enjoying the views more in descent. One fine view is found on the stile by the old cottage. Far below, next to the glinting ribbon of the Llugwy is the unmistakable outline of Cobden's. If that does not put a spring in your step, I do not know what will! So, simply retrace the route taken in ascent to a welcome pint.

Walk 20: The Eastern Carneddau

Distance: 11 miles (17.5km)

Height gained: 2790ft (850m)

Time: 6 to 7 hours.

Start: Capel Curig Car Park. GR 721582.

Terrain: Good paths, boggy at first on to high, grass covered, then rocky mountains. To complete the route as described there is one short but steep scramble, quite exposed!

Maps: OS Landranger Sheet 115 – Caernarvon & Bangor (1:50 000).

Public transport: Buses from Llandudno to Llanberis and Llanwrst to Bangor and Snowdon Sherpa buses in season.

The Bryn Tyrch, Capel Curig; tel: (01690) 720223

As with walk No. 19, the best starting place is the public car park a short distance from the chosen watering hole. The Bryn, as it is usually known, is however, worth the few minutes' walk it will take from the village, even at the end of a long day. This is a walkers' bar. Comfortable and cozy, nobody is going to mind if you are dressed in hill-going clothes, and although crowded it remains welcoming. A word of warning however. At very busy times the food, which is cooked to order, can be a while in coming; mind you, the wait is worth it. Children are welcome, as are dogs in the Public Bar and garden.

The Carneddau

The Carneddau are Snowdonia's wildest and most remote mountains, culminating in the rolling Carnedd Llewellyn and Carnedd Dafydd ridge, a high plateau in excess of 3000 feet (915m), the UK's largest area of high ground outside Scotland! These eastern hills, although still substantial, give the walker a taste of their remoteness whilst remaining easily accessible from the pubs and hotels of Capel Curig. The descent from Pen-yr-Helgi-Du to the saddle, however, still requires care and a reasonable amount of competence on exposed rock, especially in the wet!

The Ogwen Valley from Tal-y-Waen

The Walk

Leave the car park, cross the River Llugwy by Joe Brown's mountaineering shop and turn left onto the A5. In about fifteen minutes, just past Bronheulog, take the signposted footpath diagonally across the meadow on the right. A feint track shows the way, until at the farm of Tal-y-Waen another sign post points the way. Just as well, as the track now becomes boggy and indistinct, crossing several leats as it heads towards the distinct gap between Pen Llithrig y Wrach and Creigiau Gleison.

After crossing a particularly wide water-course, another bridge and a stile are visible off to the left, and the track becomes a little more solid. The views from this point are spectacular, with Llyn

Cowlyd in front, and a continuous sweep of Moel Siabod (Walk No. 19) and the northern slopes of the Glydderau in the opposite direction. On the other side of the stile, the blunt ridge of Pen Llithrig y Wrach rears up, and bracken and boulders lead to a good path on the ridge.

The route to the summit is unrelenting, so it gives plenty of time to ponder on the hill's name. In English it translates as the Slippery Hill of the Witch, and on a day of scudding low clouds, it is easy to imagine the noise of the wind to be the cackling of some toothless hag! No witches are to be found on its 2622 foot (799m) top however, just a scruffy cairn and some fine views taking in several of the 3000 foot summits.

To the west lies the next objective. This time, the Hill of the Black Hound (another sinister name!) or Pen yr Helgi Du, slightly higher at 2733ft (833m). This, however, is not the full story; between lies a drop of about six hundred feet (183m), with an equal grind up the far slopes. That pub seems worlds away!

A narrow but good path is followed into the pass, although care must be taken in wet or frozen conditions, as it crosses convex grassy slopes above broken ground. As the stile on Bwlch Trimardog is approach the going relents a little and soon the saddle is reached. This is where you will regret all that downhill, as the summit of Pen yr Helgi Du is about thirty minutes stiff climb away, although it is downhill all the way from there.

This summit is much more typical of the Carneddau with shattered rocks lying all around like the scales of some huge fossilised beast, while in front are the huge cliffs of Craig yr Ysfa. These were first climbed by the Abraham Brothers in 1905, who strung together the still popular Amphitheatre Buttress. A very fine climb! The immediate interest however, is getting down to the col high above Cwm Eigiau. A narrow ridge with a big drop on either side may seem intimidating, although with care it is not as difficult as it appears. (This section can be avoided by following an easier path down Y Braich, the south ridge of Pen yr Helgi Du.) The col high above Ffynon Llugwy, with superb views to Tryfan and the Glyders, makes a great spot for a rest, however.

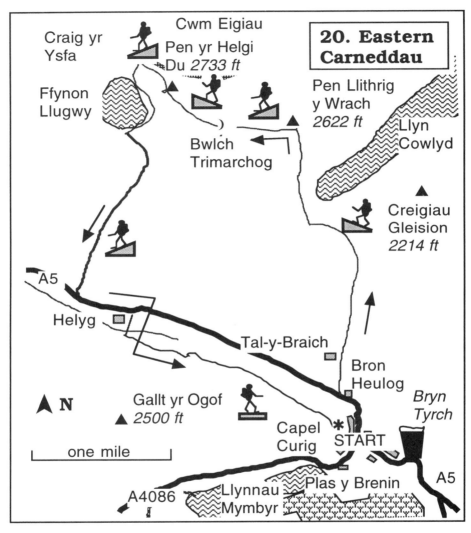

20. Eastern Carneddau

Although downhill, this is still rugged mountain terrain, and the slatey zig-zags drop very steeply at first, before easing off to a good path above the lake – this crag-girt lake is the source of the Afon Llugwy, which was crossed at the start of the walk near Joe Brown's – which is followed until it meets the metalled track at its outflow.

Turn left onto the road, and simply follow this downhill through a few gates, and out onto the A5. Now comes the really dangerous part! The A5 has to be crossed; then the footpath past Helyg, the famous Climbers' Club hut, is taken.

Fortunately the road is soon left behind, as a slightly boggy path crosses two bridges of flat rocks to join the old road that used to link Capel Curig and Bethesda. This gives easy walking back to Capel, first passing beneath the crags of Gallt yr Ogof, where the cave – or Ogof – can be seen high on the rocks. In winter, a huge icicle can form here which becomes a high standard ice-climb. Sped along by the views of the ridge so recently negotiated, the farm of Gelli is soon reached, and the Llugwy crossed again before coming out into the centre of the village.

Now for that well earned beer. Follow the A5 towards Betws-y-Coed for a short distance – admiring the views towards faraway Snowdon – and watch out for the white painted hotel on the left. The sign is unmistakable, a mountaineering mole climbing out of its hole, and just beyond again is the fast flowing river whose source we so recently visited.

Walk 21: Y Garn's Rocky Ridges

Distance: 8 miles (12.8km)

Height gained: 2990ft (912m)

Time: 5 to 7 hours.

Start: Nant Peris Car Park. GR 607582.

Terrain: Some paths are very little used especially in upper Cwm Dudodyn and the top part of Y Garn is very rocky. Descent generally safe in all conditions, although in Cwm Cneifio it can require concentration. This is a long and serious route that may need all the daylight of a short winter's day.

Maps: OS Landranger Sheet 115 – Caernarvon & Bangor (1:50 000).

Public transport: Infrequent local, and Snowdon Sherpa buses in season.

The Vaynol Arms, Nant Peris; tel: (01286) 870284

Nant Peris was, at one time, the main village at the foot of the Llanberis Pass. All that changed, however, as quarry workers moved down hill to Llanberis – the new town – for work in the enormous Dinorwic slate quarries. The Vaynol Arms is the only pub in Nant Peris, and is a well known climbers' and walkers' pub, and has a bar especially for them to the rear of the low, white building. It serves Robinsons beers and good wholesome food, and children are welcome, although dogs are not allowed inside.

Y Garn

The Western Glyderrau are far less frequented than Glyder Fawr and Glyder Fach, and even less so from the southern side. It is one of the 3000ft (915m) peaks of Wales and, being central, has good views of many of the other high mountains. It is a wild and rocky setting, but has the advantage that navigation is not too much of a problem in just about all conditions. The steep North Face will not allow for

A view to the summit of Y Garn

any mistakes, and in winter a cornice of overhanging snow can form: potentially very dangerous – although in good conditions there is no real danger. The descent can be nearly as tiring as the ascent and in places requires a high measure of concentration.

The Walk

The car park in Nant Peris forms a convenient starting point, so turn left onto the A4086 and walk past the pub and Mountain Rescue Post on the left, and the chapel on the right. Just after a small stream turn right, and before recrossing the water continue on the metalled track curving away to the left towards the rocky summit of Foel Goch. Climb steeply, until just past a solitary climbing club hut, then aim for the obvious footpath sign in front where the track is left for the open hillside.

Cross the ladder stile and follow the obvious path to another stile, then broad grass zig-zags with superb views of the Snowdon massif

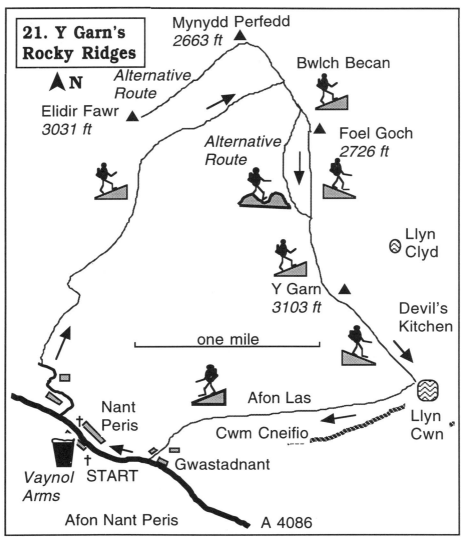

21. Y Garn's Rocky Ridges

▲ N

Mynydd Perfedd
2663 ft ▲

Bwlch Becan

Alternative Route

Elidir Fawr ▲
3031 ft

Alternative Route

▲ Foel Goch
2726 ft

⊚ Llyn
Clyd

Y Garn ▲
3103 ft

Devil's Kitchen

one mile

Afon Las

Llyn Cwn

Nant Peris

Cwm Cneifio

† Gwastadnant

Vaynol † START
Arms

Afon Nant Peris   A 4086

behind. Soon, the path and the Afon Dudodyn come together, and the way leads above the rocky defile and fence, to a rickety footbridge. This is the key to the upper cwm, although paths exist on the eastern bank – well provided with stiles – and along the high ridge bounding the eastern wall of the cwm.

Cross the bridge and follow very feint paths across a small hillock. Tiny tracks clinging tenuously to the side of the hill lead on and up towards the forbiddingly steep 'headwall' at the end of the cwm. As the stream begins to tumble down a series of cascades, so the way becomes steep and if this was not bad enough, the path disappears to boot! All the intrepid Pubhiker can do, is plod onwards, head down and cursing – or turn round and scuttle back to the Vaynol! The views of Snowdon behind almost justify this option. Almost!

Eventually the col is reached, no mistaking this as there is a fence running along the whole route. From here it is feasible to go left and climb the rocky spur of Elidir Fawr, returning via the same route – although this will add at least an hour to the walk. The easier option is to go right, and ascend rocky slopes to the top of Foel Goch (2726ft, 831m), from which there is a magnificent view of the 3103ft (946m) Y Garn in front, and the Carneddau stretching away on the other side of the Nant Ffrancon valley. (An even sneakier way is the path that contours the slopes of Foel Goch to arrive at the fence between itself and Y Garn. It is important, however, to not go too low as another path exists that requires a bit of an uphill slog to reach the same point.)

From the summit of Foel Goch, descend to cross the fence and follow the shaly zig-zags on the edge of the huge North Face of the mountain. This path climbs steeply before levelling out briefly, at which point the summit comes into view, then narrows into a rocky ridge as it approaches the summit cairn. From here all the major mountain groups of Snowdonia are laid out like a map and parts of routes 20 and 22 may clearly be seen as well as tiny Llyn Clyd in the arms of Y Garn, with Llyn Ogwen and Llyn Idwal far below. This is truly a summit to savour!

The descent is obvious in all weathers, as a well worn path leads – rockily at first – straight down the south-eastern flank of the hill to cross a fence and then dive straight for the shores of the little Llyn Cwn. From here it is worth making a short detour to the north to peer into the depths of The Devil's Kitchen, a traditional rock-climb, first ascended in 1898 and definitely not a walker's route. There is also a remarkable view of Tryfan – a 3010ft (917m) peak of solid rock, and one of the best mountains in the area to climb; sadly the lack of nearby pubs precludes it from this book.

The way back however, lies to the south, so follow the good, cairned path running between the bulk of the Glyders and Y Garn. This can be very wet on this poorly drained saddle, so pick a route avoiding the juiciest sections to a stile where the path improves. Wind across the saddle following the infant stream, and descend gently on grass slopes studded with grey boulders. High in front is the ridge along which the rack and pinion Snowdon Mountain Railway runs on its way to the summit, and the block of Halfway House Station is clearly visible. Seeing a steam train dragging its way up the ridge is perhaps a defilement of the scenery, yet also remaining an incredible sight. Just after a stile the view opens out down the Llanberis Pass and the first sight of the pub for several hours. Still a long way to go though!

The route now becomes steeper alongside the waterfall, and it is necessary to take care where the path splits. The correct way takes the left-hand branch, while the right ends abruptly above a large buttress from which it is best to retrace one's steps. Continue steeply to a few stunted trees where a small footbridge has been placed over a stream entering from the left. Just a few rocks remain; then steep grass leads to a wall which forces the path first right, then left, to another stile.

From here the way is obvious as it winds around cottages – follow the waymarked path – to finally emerge on the road again. The short distance down the road is almost pleasurable after the rigours of the descent, and feet and knees will be glad of a bit of a rest from steep rocks. Just a few minutes walking will have a pint of Robinsons clutched thankfully, and perhaps momentarily, as the long high ridges are relived. Sitting comfortably in the Climber's Bar now though, a rest well earned!

Walk 22: A Snowdon Loop

Distance: 10.1 miles (16.2km)

Height gained: 3090ft (942m)

Time: 6 to 8 hours.

Start: Rhyd Ddu car park. GR 571525.

Terrain: Generally good paths; the upper part of the mountain is very rocky and can be confusing in mist. Pleasant descent along, at times, a narrow ridge, care is needed to find the correct point for descent in poor visibility, although a foolproof option exists. This is a long and serious route that may need all the daylight of a short winter's day and should not be underestimated at any time.

Maps: OS Landranger Sheet 115 – Caernarvon & Bangor (1:50 000).

Public transport: Buses run along A4085 and Snowdon Sherpa buses in season.

The Cwellyn Arms, Rhyd Ddu; tel: (01766) 890321

A pub that claims nine Real Ales at any given time, as well as being open all day, nine days a week (yes, really!) just has to be visited. The fact that the Cwellyn Arms stands at the foot of the highest mountain in England and Wales is an added bonus. The low stone building is a welcoming Free-House with accommodation and good, very varied food. The beer choice is constantly changing and may contain some idiosyncratic and unusual ales. Children and dogs are welcome and there is also a pleasant garden and play area beside the tumbling Afon Gwyrai.

Snowdon

It must be every Pubhiker's ambition to ascend the highest and perhaps most interesting mountain in Wales still attainable from a pub. Of course, this is possible from Llanberis – you can even catch the train from there – but the chosen paths are far quieter, and more interesting to boot, than walking up the railway track! Of all the major paths on the hill, the Snowdon Ranger is thought to be the oldest, and gives a pleasant and generally less crowded way to the top, while the Rhyd Ddu path brings the thirsty, but hopefully happy walker right back to the pub! A short stretch of road or a series of footpaths link the two routes, or with two cars it is possible to leave one at Rhyd Ddu and another at Snowdon Ranger.

The Walk

From the car park, go past the pub and walk northwards along the road, it is possible to take footpaths across country to reach the Snowdon Ranger path, although I find the mile or so of road a much faster option. It is a reasonably interesting walk, with Llyn Cwellyn in front, Snowdon to the right, and the great bulk of Mynydd Mawr looming up in front, until the Snowdon Ranger youth hostel is reached on the right – here the walk proper starts!

Just beyond the hostel is a path signposted as a bridleway and a footpath, with a gate and stile, this is the Snowdon Ranger Path, said to be the oldest route up Snowdon – the Snowdon Ranger being an early guide. On a stony surface at first, it is well waymarked as it zig-zags towards the obvious house and tumbling stream. It soon becomes a more open hill path as it passes through a gate to climb gently, first one way, then the other, across the broad face of the ridge with good views towards Rhyd Ddu.

The way soon curves round to the right and the spoil tips dominate the scene before another bend and the huge shattered mass of crags surrounding Cwm Clogwyn arrest the gaze, with Llechog (along the top of which the descent route runs) off to the right. From here, the path levels out across a wet and boggy section before dropping to cross a stream, then levelling out again with the ridge of Clogwyn Du'r Arddu rearing up in front.

All that pleasant strolling alongside Llyn Ffynnon-y-gwas has a downside. This is a mountain path, it is also the highest mountain in the book and this can now only mean one thing – pain! The path is easy to follow as it climbs towards the skyline, it also rises around

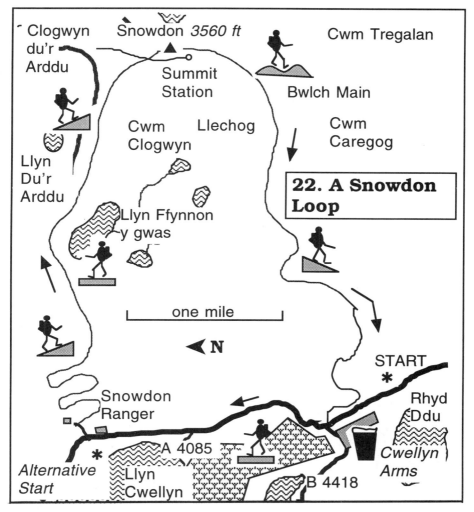

1900ft (580m) in just about a mile and a quarter, and there is soon a fence on the left to stop the hapless walker or sheep tumbling over the cliffs of Cloggy. The views now include Llanberis, far below, and the ridge followed by the mountain railway with its tiny engines puffing to the summit.

Eventually the angle begins to relent, although it is still a steady pull up shaley screes to the ridge at Bwlch Glas (3258ft, 993m) and the prominent finger stone to help walkers find the Snowdon Ranger in descent. In ascent no such aid is necessary, there is a railway line to follow! The new path alongside and above this soon speeds (?) weary boots to the very summit of Yr Wyddfa at 3560ft (1085m) where on a good day the views are nothing short of amazing. Snaking ridges, turquoise lakes and distant sea shores all combine to make a memorable sight. Most days of the year however, it seems that the only reward is greyness and the looming bulk of the Summit Station. Still, at least you can get a drink – no real ale though!

No doubt soon, the crowds will begin to get too much so descend steeply in a south, south-westerly direction to the Bwlch Main ridge high above Cwm Tregalan. Avoid the path to the left – this leads to Lliwedd and the Watkin Path – but continue along the very crest. The path twists and turns through rock towers and bouldery outcrops before forking off to the right to quit the crown. This descends alongside fences, in broad zig-zags, to reach the edge of the drop above Llechog where a wall is soon reached with a new kissing-gate built into it. Cross here and continue to the next gate along a sometimes rough path.

On the Bwlch Main ridge

From here the path descends more steeply passing through small outcrops with views over the lakes and village below, before crossing a short, cairned stretch of moorland. Continue through outcrops to a levelling with a superb view up the Nantlle Valley to the left of the crags of Craig y Bera, then just after the remains of a building to a stile and gate. This leads out to an area of tilted grey slabs, where the path again winds through before coming to another level section, again boggy, but this time blessed with flat stone laid to reduce erosion.

Just a couple of minutes later another kissing-gate leads out onto the path leading down from Bwlch Cwm Llan. (If the ridge from Snowdon summit is not left at the correct point, or in mist, it is possible to continue to this col between the ridge and the peak of Yr Aran and descend through the dissused quarries on the west side of the mountain.) However, from the gate turn right and follow the broad track gently downwards. Well surfaced, it soon comes to a long deserted quarry and a gate. From here it is just a couple of minutes stroll through the houses of Rhyd Ddu to the Cwellyn Arms.

The Yorkshire Dales

Yorkshire is justly famous for both its walking and its beer. Most of the walking to interest the hill-walker is, however, in North Yorkshire, in the Dales National Park, where the Three Peaks – Ingleborough, Pen-y-Ghent and Whernside are to be found. The traverse of all three is a well-known challenge. The landscape is a mixture of gritstone and limestone – here are to be found high moorlands, and around the Craven Fault, deep scars and bare limestone. Erosion of the limestone has produced the caves and pot-holes for which the area is famous, as well as the remarkable limestone pavements, such as that found high above Malham Cove.

Covering about 680 square miles, no other landscape combines the wild and the domestic quite so well, the heights contrasting ideally with the lush river valleys. Furthermore, no hill-area has quite so much evidence of man; everywhere are stone barns and farmhouses, and the dry-stone walls sometimes reach to the very heights of the fell. Crossed by the Pennine Way, the walking is varied and interesting, and the three walks in this book have been selected to take in as many of these varieties as possible. There are two walks in Wensleydale, one on either side of the valley, and one in Upper Wharfedale. Within their 33.1 miles (53km) lie limestone heights, moorland and quiet riverside paths as well as the highest waterfall in England.

The Yorkshire Dales are also an important part of popular literature, with James Herriot's books and TV series being based there. As well as the 'Herriot Trail', there are plenty of other interesting places to visit within its beautiful area with many ancient buildings, show caves and natural sights all adding up to a great walking holiday location. Of course, everywhere there is to be found that wonderful ale!

There are also approximately 16 independent breweries in the county of North Yorkshire alone (close to 43 in the whole of Yorkshire) giving an unrivalled selection of local beers. Apart from the Green Dragon Inn in the tiny hamlet of Hardraw (Walk 23) the other two walks offer a choice of drinking houses, and in the case of the walk starting from Hawes, several. This means that pubs other than those featured may be enjoyed, along with their variety of ales. From nationally famous Theakston's and Samuel Smith's – the county's oldest – to newcomers such as Daleside and Black Sheep, the choice seems endless. What better reason for working up a thirst?

All three routes in this section appear on just one OS map, Sheet 98, Wensleydale and Upper Wharfedale.

Walk 23: Great Shunner Fell

Distance: 10.6 miles (17km)

Height gained: 1561ft (476m)

Time: 4 to 5 hours.

Start: Hardraw, Pennine Way. GR 866912.

Terrain: Good paths, generally well signposted at lower levels, pathways laid across wet moorland when approaching the summit.

Maps: OS Landranger Sheet 98 – Wensleydale and Upper Wharfedale (1:50 000).

Public transport: Buses to Hawes.

Green Dragon Inn, Hardraw; tel: (01969) 667392

The tiny Dales hamlet of Hardraw is famous for the waterfall of Hardraw Force, the highest above-ground waterfall in England, which is situated in the 14 acre grounds of the 16th century Green Dragon Inn. The pub is a large stone building with a wonderful warm atmosphere serving Theakston's ales and excellent food – both children and dogs are made welcome. They also have available rooms in the pub or self-catering accommodation.

Great Shunner Fell

At 2348ft (716m), Great Shunner Fell is the loftiest walk in this section. It is also the only walk in the book for which the same route is recommended for ascent and descent. This fortunately is no hardship, as the views are incredible, that from the summit even reaching to the Lake District, and the hill seems to offer a quite different character in descent. It takes the form of a huge curving whale-back and is a prominent landmark on the northern side of Wensleydale, especially when viewed from Hawes or Appersett.

With the Buttertubs Pass on one side, and Cotterdale on the other, the strangely beacon-crowned ridge is isolated from the surrounding fells, and a traverse to Thwaite makes an admirable expedition if transport can be arranged.

The Walk

From the road take the gravel-surfaced bridleway signposted to Thwaite, Cotterdale and Fossdale Moss; this is the Pennine Way. At first, the way climbs gradually within walls, winding sinuously into the open countryside. Just to the right are the trees surrounding the famous waterfall, Hardraw Force. Where the path curves to the left, the views begin to open out, and distant vehicles may be seen labouring up the initial climb of the Buttertubs Pass, while in front, the obvious path may be seen climbing the long ridge of the fell.

At the wall, where there is a gate and a ladder stile, a vague track leads off to the right, while the main path is signposted as the Pennine Way and curves to the left. From here there is a superb panorama of Wether and Dodd Fells (see walk No. 25), while a little further on, where the footpath to Cotterdale branches off, there are fine views of Ingleborough. Still climbing steadily, the scene just gets more wild, with the broad expanse of fell on the right broken by the deep depression of Hearne Beck.

Just before the final wall a couple of small scars of limestone protrude from the fell and a gate and stile lead onto the open hillside. Continue along the Pennine Way – now less steeply – along the massive broad ridge, curving round as far as the eye can see. The path is now more typically upland, a mixture of rocks and grass, with, to the left, the forested slopes around Garsdale stretching away. As it climbs it enters a landscape of dark moorland scattered with the wind-eroded shapes of gritstone, quite a contrast to the white limestone!

In places the flat slabs of grit form a natural pavement through the peat, although further on, wooden 'pallets' have been laid to help the walker across boggy areas. It soon rises into an area of peat hags, where gritstone flags have been laid to carry the path through a

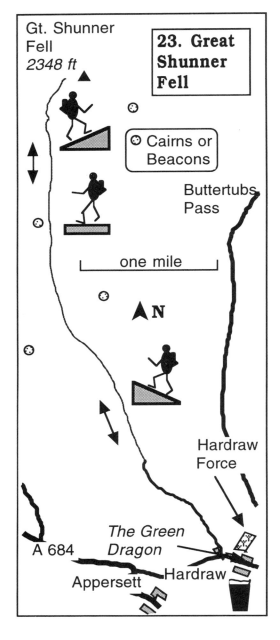

Gt. Shunner
Fell
2348 ft

**23. Great
Shunner
Fell**

☺ Cairns or
Beacons

Buttertubs
Pass

one mile

▲ N

Hardraw
Force

*The Green
Dragon*
A 684
Appersett   Hardraw

typical Pennine land-
scape of tussocky yel-
low grass and expanses
of waving Cotton Grass.

After a long level sec-
tion through moorland
there is a final little pull
up a grassy slope to re-
veal more moorland
leading to a second 'fi-
nal little pull'. This second one leads to a big
cairn with views across
another large expanse
of moorland – to the fin-
gers of stone eerily situated on the open moor
to the right, and a bea-
con on the end of the
ridge. The path then
leads across flat moor-
land to yet another 'fi-
nal little pull' up to the
broad ridge.

The way across this
stretch is predomi-
nantly flagged with yel-
low-topped posts
indicating the route – it
is important to stick to
the recommended path
to minimise erosion.
The manufactured path
crosses peat hags and
on to a 'final little pull'
up an almost com-

pletely paved and stepped rise. This leads onto a very eroded section of boggy moorland, again level, and again surfaced with gritstone flags. This, though really is it, and the cairn and trig-point are now clearly visible in front.

Across a sheep fence the rounded top of the fell is soon reached and the views are quite superb. Into Swaledale, across to Wild Boar Fell at the end of the Howgills and even far into the blue hills of the Lake District while nearby are the strange monoliths known simply as The Pile of Stones. This is truly a place to rest and savour the panorama and to this end a wind shelter is being erected on the summit. All too soon, the heights have to be quit and it is time to start downhill.

Although there does seem to be a way down crossing the peat atop the fell and dropping into the depression between Fossdale Moss and Great Shunner Fell, this is not recommended. Firstly, there is no right of way across the top of the fell, and secondly the path up Hearne ends at the mine workings, and is very difficult to follow even from below – being little used. So all that remains is to retrace the line of ascent.

This is no hardship as the views are, if anything, even more impressive in descent and the path soon drops from the windswept summit to the shelter of the peat groughs. Just twenty minutes lead to the end of the 'pavements', so toil across on the upward route, the view of Inglebourough's flat summit constantly ahead. All those 'final little pulls' pass unnoticed as the brown uplands contrast with the brighter greens of Wensleydale spread out in front. A delightful hour's walking leads to the intake wall and the start of the track back to Hardraw.

After the darkness of the peat and gritstone, the gleaming limestone and brighter pastoral scenery is a pleasant change. With Ingleborough on the skyline and Hawes in the valley the track provides easy and fast walking back to the road, where a left leads over the beck to the welcoming Green Dragon.

Before resting however, pay the 60p (1997), and take the walk up to Hardraw Force. Winding through woodland, with the stream on the right, soon has the roar of the fall growing in volume. Then,

The view from behind Hardraw Force

rounding a bend, the full impact of the waterfall is in front. A continuous and unbroken drop from the lip of a small cirque with a large overhang has the body of water falling well clear of the rock. A feint path may be seen leading behind the water, although it is prohibited to cross behind the fall. If it were not, however, a path could be reached along the other side of the beck passing a couple of ruined buildings and head back to the pub. It is also possible to cross the stream bed just below the pool to reach the same spot.

Walk 24: Buckden Pike

Distance: 8.4 miles (13.4km)

Height gained: 1647ft (502m)

Time: 4 to 5 hours.

Start: Buckden car park. GR 942775.

Terrain: Good paths, generally well signposted. One short section of path is not a Right of Way, although it is well trodden. Finish via the easy riverside path.

Maps: OS Landranger Sheet 98 – Wensleydale & Upper Wharfedale (1:50 000).

Public transport: Buses run to Buckden.

Fox and Hounds, Starbotton; tel: (01756) 760269

This walk is particularly well endowed with pubs, the Buck Inn at the start, and the 400 year old building of the Fox and Hounds (which has been a pub for 160 years), a couple of miles before the end of the route in the tiny hamlet of Starbotton. This is the recommended pub, CAMRA listed and offering fine food and accommodation in a relaxed and convivial atmosphere where walkers and their children are welcome. There is also a small garden where dogs are allowed. One pleasant aspect of the pub is the no-smoking dining area just off the cosy bar.

Buckden Pike

Although really just a continuation of the high 'ridge' leading to Great Whernside, Buckden Pike (2302ft, 702m) is a worthy walk in its own right. The views on the ascent reach right up Bishopdale, while those on the way down are of Upper Wharfedale, enhanced by the delightful Cam Gill Beck on the left. The actual fell-top is open moorland giving sweeping vistas across to Pen-y-Ghent and beyond, while the walk finishes with a pastoral path alongside the winding River Wharfe.

The Walk

A gate in the top left-hand corner of the car park leads easily onto the fell via the slanting Buckden Rake. Gentle climbing on a good stony track soon reaches an area of small limestone scars on the right, as the fine trees begin to recede on the downhill side. At a second gate the path splits and the track to Buckden Pike is sign-posted diagonally across a pasture, to the obvious gate. At the upper gate may be found a few flat rocks where it is pleasant to sit and rest whilst admiring the views.

Where the path enters the National Trust area is a plaque showing the extent of the NT property, and the path now takes on a more 'upland' character. A grassy swathe cuts across the fell-side to the obvious rim of crags and a stream crossing. It is possible now to trace

Buckden Rake and Upper Wensleydale

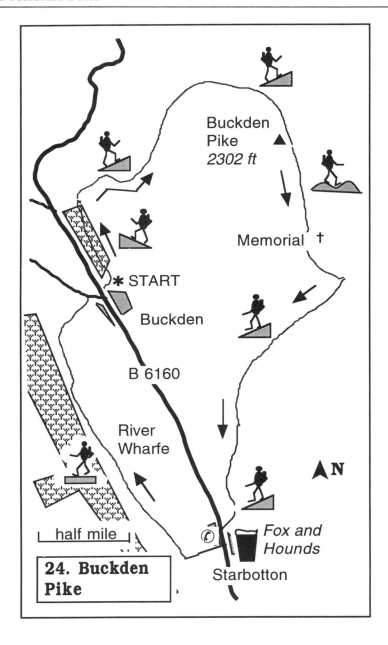

Buckden
Pike
2302 ft

Memorial †

START

Buckden

B 6160

River
Wharfe

half mile

**24. Buckden
Pike**

Fox and
Hounds

Starbotton

N

the route as it climbs obliquely through the gaps in the walls via a tottering mass of limestone crags.

After another gate it is time to turn away from the views and start the straight ascent of the fell with the final slopes rearing up in front. This is now on the gritstone cap atop the hill and the paths weave through a wet area towards a wall. Here, a finger-post points up an eroded track, climbing as steeply as anything yet met. This leads to another levelling, after which the wall begins to curve to the right and the first welcome sight of the white trig-point marking the end of the climbing. The rounded top of the fell is also decorated with a cairn and pole a little further to the west.

A ladder stile crosses the wall surrounding the NT land and a good path – though not a right of way – leads more or less southwards towards Great Whernside. This can be boggy in places as it skirts the newly-rebuilt wall on a sweeping expanse of moor. Just a few minutes walking brings the poignant memorial to a Polish aircrew who perished in 1942 when their Wellington bomber crashed here. Still wired to the cross is a small piece of tangled air-frame; a fitting tribute in a setting of wilderness and freedom.

Almost immediately after the cross, a gap in the wall on the right marks the start of the track across Starbotton Fell. It is pleasant to be walking on a sound surface, and to enjoy views across Wharfdale again, until at another broken-down wall the path emerges onto the open hill-side. Cam Gill Beck, now in its deep ravine is to the left, as the path loses height rapidly on the obvious path. Although in places it can be boggy, it is always easy to follow as it drops steeply then contours above the beck. This whole area is alive with rabbits as they scurry away from your approach.

The path levels, and a lone bridleway sign stands amid a high area of upland, pointing up, and down the slope. Height is lost to a gate and stile where the way undulates across grassland on a springy turf path before becoming a stony farm track. As it starts to bear leftwards the Wharfe comes into view and a very steep descent is made to the beck and a right turn to the village where the welcoming Fox and Hounds gives chance for the toes to recover and the knees to stop creaking.

Refreshed, turn left along the road to a sign to Arncliffe, Kettlewell and Buckden, and follow the walled lane leading towards the steep slopes of Firth Fell. At a bridge across the river, turn right towards Buckden. This is part of the Dales Way; bridges and all manner of stiles carry the path alongside the river until the Wharfe meanders away. Cross pastures and join the National Trust's Upper Wharfedale property to where the river rejoins. A short distance along a gravel drive, take the signposted footpath branching off to the right.

This basically follows the line of the river, and the path is marked by yellow tipped posts and a multitude of stiles (the sheer number will probably have doubled the total amount of ascent!) before reaching the stone bridge where a squeeze leads out to the road. A final short uphill stretch leads to the village green, a stone's throw from the Buck Inn and the car park. The tiny Post Office offers a potentially new experience in the shape of home-made (non-alcoholic!) Nettle Beer. Just the thing on a hot day!

Walk 25: A Hawes Horseshoe

Distance: 14.1 miles (22.5km)

Height gained: 1410ft (430m)

Time: 5 to 7 hours.

Start: Parking in Hawes centre.

Terrain: Generally good paths although some on Wether Fell can be a little difficult to follow. Very short stretch of road and some byways, including a stretch of the Pennine Way.

Maps: OS Landranger Sheet 98 – Wensleydale & Upper Wharfedale (1:50 000).

Public transport: Plentiful buses run through Hawes.

The Crown, Hawes; tel: (01969) 667212

Hawes is blessed with several pubs serving traditional ales, many in its Market Square (market day Tuesday). The Crown is a welcoming, stone-built hostelry serving Theakston's Ales in a comfortable and warm environment. Food is available at the usual times and children are welcome inside, although dogs are not allowed further than the pleasant outdoor seating area – where there is always a bowl of water for those that do not like Old Peculiar!

Wether and Dodd Fells

The great bulk of Wether Fell rises behind Hawes in a massive dark mass reaching 2014ft (614m), and on the other side of the narrow mountain road into Gayle is Dodd Fell at 2191ft (668m). This walk visits the top of neither, but does encounter some varied and dramatic countryside nonetheless. It also affords superb views of Ingleborough and returns to the delightful hamlet of Gayle via a very scenic section of the Pennine Way.

The Walk

From Hawes market place, set off in an easterly direction and cross the tumbling Gayle Beck, before, just past a small crescent, there is a gate in the wall and a footpath sign to Burtersett. This is paved with gritstone slabs and crosses a pasture, with high on the right the aerial festooned Yorburgh (1689ft, 515m). Through a squeeze is the road and the path continues via a stile, again across meadows and more squeezes to the road to Burtersett, where a right turn is made. Climb gently uphill to the little stone-built hamlet nestling beneath Burtersett High Pasture.

At a left-hand bend – there is a small green and a seat – turn right down the no-through road to the bridleway leading past some houses and out onto the open hillside. Great sweeping curves on a

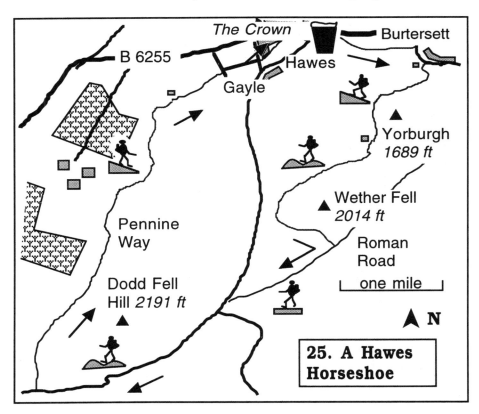

The Crown   Burtersett

B 6255   Hawes

Gayle

Yorburgh
1689 ft

Pennine
Way

Wether Fell
2014 ft

Roman
Road

Dodd Fell
Hill *2191 ft*

one mile

▲ N

**25. A Hawes
Horseshoe**

rough farm track ease the way up the hill, and towards the obvious mass of Yorburgh, guarded by its ring of limestone. After a couple of gates, the way is signposted to the Roman Road and there are excellent views of Upper Wensleydale, with just to the right the path up Great Shunner Fell (walk 23).

A wilder panorama opens out as height is gained until, just on a level with the top of Yorburgh, an old tin roofed barn is passed where a gap in the wall carries the path into a tussocky area of untamed moorland, and soon may be found a jumbled mass of limestone. An ideal place to stop for a rest, or continue through the gap and turn right parallel to the wall and proceed to a prominent cairn, where may be found a small rocky amphitheatre.

On the Roman Road, Wether Fell

Now contouring the fellside, the path passes through an area of sinks and evidence of long-abandoned mines. Always alongside the wall – there are now excellent views into Sleddale – the path curves to the left, with Ingleborough looming up ahead, and continues to the semi-surfaced Roman Road overlooking Semer Water. Turn right here, continue to a gate and the motor-road and turn left, until this can be quit for the continuation of the Roman Road at a sharp bend. Gated, this is signposted to

Cam Houses, and it gives a roller coaster of a walk above the dark expanse of Cam Woodlands.

With Dodd Fell on one side, and Oughtershawside on the other this gives easy walking around the 1900ft (580m) contour for over two miles, until at a gate the Pennine Way is reached. From here Hawes is signposted down the 'white road' on the right. It is a pleasure to quit the Roman Road, although it is worth remembering that the track so recently joined, does itself carry full vehicular rights. The track clings to the rounded shoulder of fell as it contours high above Snaizeholme with its tiny farm buildings gathered around the beck.

It undulates alongside a wall until a view of Wether Fell opens out on the right. This is at Ten End, and a path (PW) is signposted off to the right. It climbs at first on close-grazed turf, then levels beside several sinks to a broken wall and a gate. The descent begins on a surprisingly undamaged path guided by the occasional cairn to a ladder stile and gate with a view down to Gayle and Hawes. A final and steep downhill leads to a new gate at Gaudy House where a farm track guides the walk back toward civilisation.

At a metalled road, turn left, then right where it is possible to follow the Pennine Way route or walk into the picturesque village of Gayle itself. In Gayle, turn left, and walk downhill to the Wensleydale Creamery with its visitor centre, then follow the path leading diagonally across pasture-land with the dark church tower to the right. This leads pleasantly in just a few minutes to the car park and the market square of Hawes and, of course, The Crown.

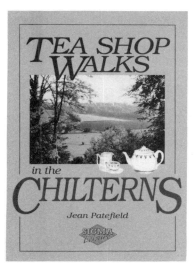

WALKS WITH CHILDREN

Another new series, this time aimed at young walkers and their parents. Simple maps are provided (so that the grown-ups don't get lost!) and there are plenty of questions (and answers) about what to look for in the countryside. The well-planned walks include 'escape routes'. Areas covered include:

Cheshire
Devon
Gloucestershire
Lake District
Peak District
Yorkshire Dales

£7.95

WALKS IN MYSTERIOUS PLACES!

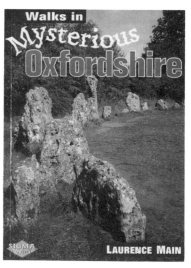

Our "Mysterious Walks" series explores the folk history of Britain — ghosts, ley lines, ancient stone circles, witchcraft and old country traditions — all with the benefit of excellent walks to reach the parts that car drivers never see!
Areas covered include:
Devon
Hampshire
Oxfordshire
South Lakeland
Wales

£6.95

(We publish many more books on English folklore and heritage)

TOWN AND VILLAGE DISCOVERY TRAILS

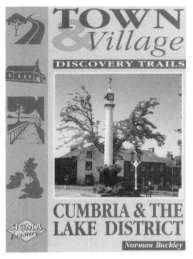

These are for walkers with shoes, not boots. Some of the most attractive towns and villages of England are covered, enabling the visitor on foot to discover what car drivers and fast-paced ramblers often miss. Areas include:

Cumbria & The Lake District
Cheshire
Cotswolds
Peak District
Staffordshire
Warwickshire
Yorkshire Dales

£6.95

50 CLASSIC WALKS IN LANCASHIRE

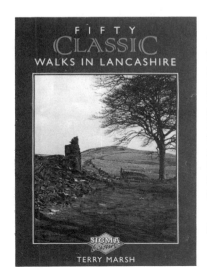

This sequel to "50 Classic Walks in the Pennines" takes walkers through the much neglected, and far-reaching, county of Lancashire. There are many fine expanses of good walking country and places of beauty within the county's boundaries — known to the locals but waiting to be discovered by the wider population. With a map to accompany each walk, his own photographs and a comprehensive index, Terry Marsh again shares his vast experience.

£8.95

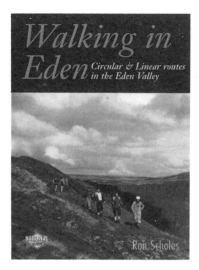

WALKING IN EDEN

This is a collection of linear and circular walks in the Eden Valley in Northern England, written by Ron Scholes – a well-known author and photographer. The five main sections, packed with historical and local interest, include: a 12-mile route to Nine-Standards Rigg from Kirkby Stephen; a 9-mile stroll alongside the peaceful River Eden; 13 miles around Cross Fell and Wildboar Scar; visits to Long Meg and Her Daughters, King Arthur's Round Table and the city of Carlisle.

£6.95

PEAK DISTRICT MEMORIES:
the photographs of E. Hector Kyme

Roger Redfern

E. Hector Kyme (1906-1987) was a renowned photographer whose work appeared in a wide range of publications. His great love was the countryside, high hills and farming life. He knew the Peak District intimately, from a lifetime of cycling and walking there. Roger Redfern, a long time friend of the photographer, has selected a representative sample of photographs taken over the last thirty years of Hector Kyme's life to form this fascinating view of the Peak District National Park and adjacent fringes. Superb photographs and entertaining text make this truly a collector's item.

£9.95

For further details of these and many more fine books, please contact:

Sigma Leisure, 1 South Oak Lane, Wilmslow, Cheshire SK9 6AR
Phone: 01625-531035; Fax: 01625-536800; E-mail: sigma.press@zetnet.co.uk

Free catalogue. ACCESS and VISA orders welcome – 24 hour Answerphone service!
Most orders are despatched on the day we receive your order – you could be enjoying our books in just a couple of days. Please add £2 p&p to all orders.